D1128468

A HANDBOOK FOR CONTEMPORARY PHOTOGRAPHY

Arnold Gassan, Assistant Professor, Ohio University

THIRD EDITION: MARCH, 1974.

HANDBOOK COMPANY, ATHENS, OHIO, 45701

DISTRIBUTED BY *LIGHT IMPRESSIONS,* BOX 3012, ROCHESTER, NEW YORK, 14614:

(Please address orders, queries about discounts, and sales requests directly to the distributor.)

Handbook Company, Box 491, Athens, Ohio 45701.
ISBN 0-912808-00-4

As a supplementary text, see *A Chronology of Photography, a critical survey of photography as a medium of art,* available from Light Impressions Corporation.

PREFACE

The contemporary camera permits almost anyone to make a photograph. It frees us to concentrate on the photographic image, its meaning, and its possibilities. But this can delude the beginner into believing he is controlling craft when the reverse is true.

The contemporary photographic print requires a complex technology. This technology can too easily master the artist; it should remain a partner in the making of photographs. If the creative vision is to be free, the process of photography must be subservient to the artist. Photographic seeing controls craft in expressive photography.

The photographic print is unique in both its richness and in its delicacy. No other medium can match the richness of the continuous tonal scale from black to white. The illusion of reality is stronger with the photograph than with any other print. But physically the print is frail—it can be weakened by chemical attack or destroyed by the least mishandling.

The print can be an end in itself; or a starting place, one from which other print statements are reached. This *Handbook* details working processes leading to other print statements. All the processes outlined have been validated in the *Graduate Photographic Processes* class at Ohio University. There are often departures in this text from methods described in older references. These departures arise from using contemporary materials.

A NOTE OF THANKS to D. James Dee for his assistance and research work with the collotype process; to John Carson Graves for the hours of careful work spent producing the parametric information offered here; and to Dr. James Wilson of Ohio University for his continued support and assistance.

TABLE OF CONTENTS

3: ADVANCED PROCESSES

response and critique methods may be carried into the field and applied while photographs are being made. photo: George McCullough

1: basic processes

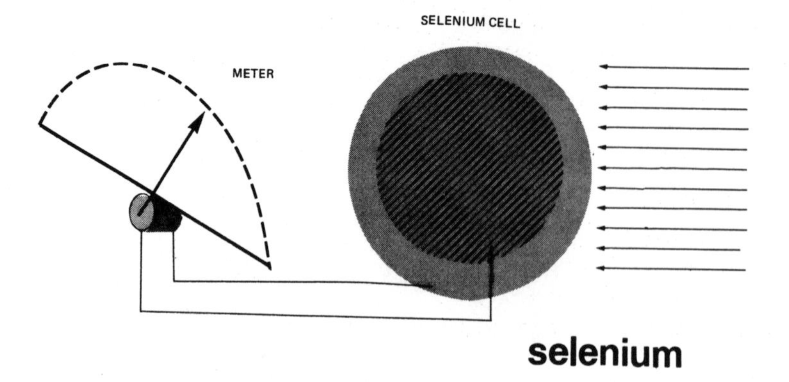

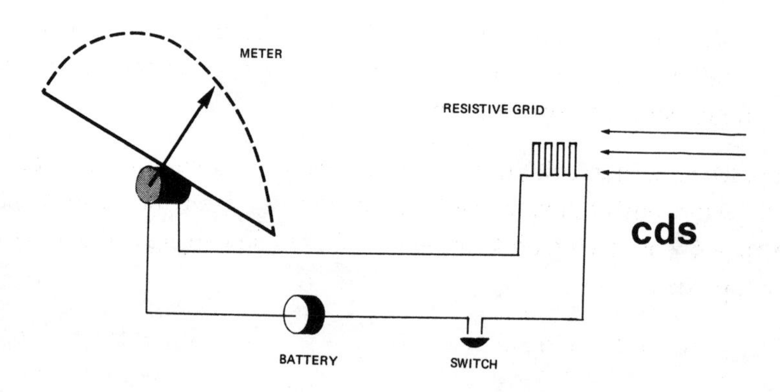

FIGURE 1·1 meters

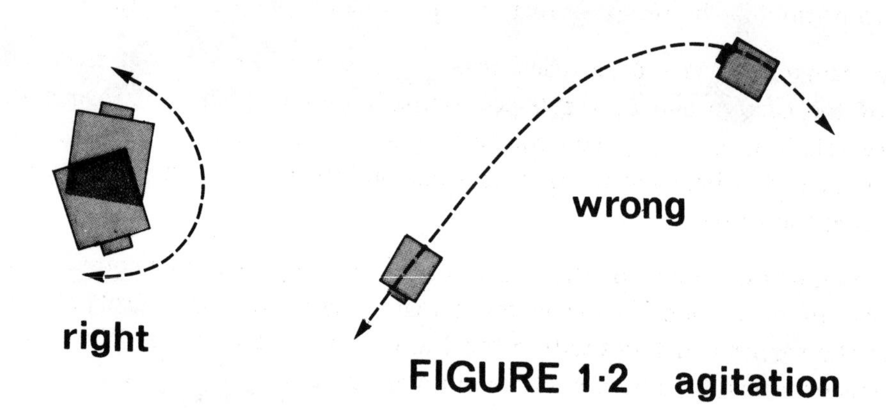

FIGURE 1·2 agitation

THE CAMERA

A contemporary camera has a lens; a way to focus the lens to form an image; a mechanism to hold the film during the exposure and to change the film between exposures; and a way to allow the photographer to see what the lens will see.

There are three main types of camera in use. These are the view camera, the rangefinder, and the reflex camera. They differ most in the means provided for seeing what the camera will photograph. Cameras vary in size depending on the size negative they expose.

Each photographer has a different feeling about the relationship between himself and his subject. The camera he uses will modify this relationship.

Each type of camera requires practice to be fully useful. The camera becomes fitted to the hand, and modifies the photographer's vision. The size of the camera and the way the image is presented affects the way it is used; the size of the film affects the representational quality of the image. The small camera encourages a direct participation in the actions being recorded. The view camera encourages a slower way of working.

The view camera presents a blank field—the groundglass. The image appears on this field when the lens is opened. Work with the view camera tends to be careful and rather slow. The image is assembled, in effect, by observing and arranging. The small camera encourages a participation with the instant of action.

The view camera requires a darkcloth. This should be large, fully opaque, and flexible. The commercial darkcloths are too stiff and too small. A good cloth can be assembled from two layers of densely woven black cotton and one layer of a light-colored cloth. These should not be stiff. Many modern fabrics have chemicals in them that leave them inflexible and these materials should be avoided. The darkcloth should be as wide as the bolt of material and about four feet long. This cloth can be bundled about the head and the camera, preventing light from spoiling the response to the dim image on the groundglass.

A view camera exacts special disciplines. The photographer ought to be able to adjust the parts of the camera and of the tripod without removing his head from the darkcloth. The primary relationship is between the photographer's eye and the groundglass image. This is stronger than that between the photographer and the physical object in front of the lens when composing the image.

The conscious assemblage of the image on the groundglass can be compared with the work of a painter or printmaker. Moving the camera, the tripod, and perhaps even the subject all change the shapes and tones within the frame of the groundglass. With the view camera the problems of a possible photograph can be worked out.

The slowness of working with a view camera also encourages the discovery of other print possibilities.

Small cameras suggest different ways of working which are responses to the nature of the camera. The reflex camera is allied both to the view camera and to the rangefinder type. The physical characteristics determine the kind of image a camera will easily produce.

The rangefinder camera encourages the photographer to use the camera as though it were an extension of his eye. He learns to anticipate most problems of graphics, then raise the camera to intercept this vision. Jockeying to find a position is often validation of his initial perception.

The reflex camera can be used like a view camera or like a rangefinder camera. In the small camera the groundglass image is not isolated from the physical subject before the camera due to the small image size.

EXPOSING FILM

No matter what camera is used certain practical problems arise. These include:

a. determining the exposure.
b. planning the development of the film.
c. printing the negative

The exposure determines the amount of photographic detail that can appear in the dark shadowed areas of the subject, as seen in the print.

There are four ways to determine exposure:

1. With an exposure table (included with each carton of film).
2. By experience or trial-and-error.
3. By using a handheld lightmeter.
4. By using a lightmeter built into the camera.

Exposure Table. The data sheet included with each carton of film is quite accurate when used on the eastern seaboard, in the midwest, or on the Pacific seaboard. It is not accurate in high country because the turbidity and water vapor that moderate the light in low lands is absent.

Trial-and-Error. This is a supplement for the data sheet or a meter of any sort. After working with a given film for a time a photographer will discover he can estimate the exposure accurately. Learning the limits of his knowledge, and of his eye, is the hard part of trial-and-error metering. The human eye is very suggestible. At twilight, or when we move rapidly

from a brightly to a dimly lighted area, the eye fails to respond accurately. One either sees more or less light than is actually present.

Memorizing the lighting conditions that produce certain exposures and that suggest certain development plans is good. It helps increase understanding of the basic controls and it simplifies routine work.

EXPOSURE METERS

The *photo generative meter* measures an electrical current generated when light strikes the cell (see Figure 1-1). It uses a selenium cell to create the current. It was the standard meter until the 1960's and is still in use. It is dependable and accurate, although it is relatively insensitive in dim light.

Light is measured by focusing it on the photosensitive cell. The cell changes the light energy into electrical energy. The electrical energy turns the armature of a small meter movement. The armature supports a pointer which indicates an exposure. On some meters the pointer moves across a dial marked in numbers that refer to actual amounts of light (either *lumens* or *candle-power/square foot*). On most meters the dial numbers are arbitrary, and therefore they apply only to that meter. Because of the differing number systems, the measurements described in the *Handbook* refer to the *exposures* rather than to the numbers taken from the meter dial. The exposures are interchangeable from one meter to another; the dial numbers are not.

Meters are designed to measure either the light reflecting from the subject—the light that the camera actually uses to make the picture; or the light falling on the subject. The first kind is a *reflected-light meter* and is the meter discussed here. The other type is an *incident-light meter*. It is traditionally popular with filmmakers. The cameraman controls the lighting ratio (i.e., the difference between the brightest and darkest areas in the picture) in film work. Expressive photography is much more concerned with the found subject matter than it is with the assembled studio scene, therefore the reflective meter is more useful. In effect it measures the light actually used by the lens of the camera, not the total light available.

The color of the light is important. The angle at which the meter is held relative to the camera and the subject is also important.

The color of light is related to the whiteness of it. Film is not equally sensitive to different colors of light. Nor are light meters. The eye accepts light of different colors as "white" when they are, in fact, quite different. Coastal daylight, rainy days, and mountain noonlight all seem white to the eye; so do tungsten and fluorescent artificial lights. Yet all are different.

Film is usually slightly less sensitive to red light than it is to blue light. Meters are made to produce correct exposure indications with coastal light that is "white". Mountain light is quite blue, and less exposure will be needed than the meter indicates. Where the light is red (as with sunsets or with tungsten light) more exposure will be needed. The amount less and more is between one-half and one stop correction.

The meter must be aimed from the same direction as the camera. Photographic subjects that are curved or cylindrical reflect light more in one direction than another. Texture influences light reflection too. If the camera and the meter view the subject from different directions they may record different amounts of light.

The light reflected from the surface of the subject is what is photographed. The film makes a record of this light. The light itself is the subject of the photograph. This light must be measured carefully to provide the best exposure.

A handheld meter may see more or less light than the camera lens sees even when they are held side by side. Meters often have wide angles of view. To measure a certain area the meter must be held close to that area, yet not shadow it. A Weston meter, for example, safely measures an 8 × 10 inch area when held about seven inches away. Held further away, it may also measure the light reflected from objects next to the card. New meters have optical aiming devices to encourage accurate metering.

Almost all meters are calibrated to provide correct exposures when they are used to measure the light reflected from a "grey" card. This is a standard color of grey. It reflects 18% of the light falling on it. Sets of standard cards are sold by Kodak.

By comparison, white typing paper reflects about 90% of the light; cheap black construction paper about 5%.

Newer meters differ in that the cell itself does not generate electricity (see Figure 1-1). In the newer cells the electricity is supplied by batteries. The cell changes its electrical resistance when light falls on it. The more light, the less resistance. As the resistance decreases, more current flows through the circuit. In operation, the *photoresistive meter* is used in the same way as a photogenerative meter.

The photoresistive meter uses a grid of cadmium sulfide (CdS) to measure the light. This grid is quite small. By increasing the battery voltage, sensitivity can be increased. These two properties permit the design of meters located within the camera—meters that measure the light actually passing through the camera lens.

The CdS cell has physical problems. The cell's sensitivity changes when it is stored in darkness for a long period of time orwhen it is exposed to very bright light. The dark-effect will increase sensitivity; this may cause it to indicate an inaccurate exposure. The cell can be returned to normal sensitivity by exposing it to normal working light for several minutes. Point it at a moderately bright surface. Turn the meter switch on and off several times.

If the meter has been accidentally pointed at the sun or another very bright light, a desensitization may occur. This means that the meter provides low exposure indications. Allow the cell to rest for 10 to 20 minutes before trusting it.

USING THE METER

Meters are made to measure 18% grey cards. If a meter is pointed at a surface which reflects more of the light, more exposure must be given to produce a correct negative. If the meter is pointed at a less reflective darker surface, less exposure must be given than indicated by the meter.

The fact that the meter is made to accurately measure only a grey card causes most of the problems for beginners in photography. If the meter is aimed at any other surface or tone, the indicated exposure must be interpreted.

Subject	Exposure correction
deep shadows	two *f*-stops less than the indicated exposure
dark objects	one *f*-stop less than the indicated exposure
middle grey—grey card	use the indicated exposure
skin tones	one *f*-stop more than the indicated exposure
concrete	two *f*-stops more than the indicated exposure
white walls	three *f*-stops more than the indicated exposure

If the most important large area in the picture which must be naturalistically rendered is skin, it may be simplest to point the meter there. Be certain the meter is not shadowing the area and that it is pointing in the same direction that the camera is looking. The actual exposure should be one *f*-stop more than the exposure indicated on the meter because skin is twice as reflective as the grey card the meter is made to measure (and calculate the exposure for) directly.

Common physical equivalents of the subjects listed above are shown in the following table.

Subject	Common physical equivalents
deep shadows	under shrubbery, inside open doors, under cars
dark objects	blue-jeans, dark clothing, brown hair
middle grey	grey card, average grassy fields, Negro skin
skin tones	sandpiles, clear north sky, highway concrete
concrete	blond hair, cloudy-bright skies
white walls	white clothing, men's shirts, white paper

The term "stop" or "*f*-stop" is used in the *Handbook* to indicate a doubling or halving of the exposure. This is done by changing the aperture one *f*-number or changing the shutter control one position. On all contemporary cameras moving the aperture from one setting to the next will change the amount of light that can pass through the lens by a factor of two. Changing the shutter speed one position will accomplish the same thing.

For example, changing from *f*-11 to *f*-16 will halve the light. Changing from 1/30th of a second to 1/60th of a second will halve the light. Either can be called *reducing the light by a stop*, i.e., by a factor of two. Increasing the exposure by a stop would be opening up the aperture (e.g., *f*-11 to *f*-8) or slowing the shutter speed (e.g., 1/30th to 1/15th of a second).

Meter readings indicate only that light is present. If the meter is pointed at a polished mirror surface (e.g., chrome, water, windows) the reading may be meaningless if the light source is included in the view. Direct or mirrored sources usually print white. There is no variation within white in the print, although the eye is capable of seeing different levels of brightness when the sources are observed directly.

Most of the time the bright and dark areas of the picture average out and the total amount of light reflected is quite close to what would have been reflected by a grey card. Because of this it is generally possible to use a meter by simply pointing it at the subject and accepting the indicated exposure.

Using the meter as though all the bright and dark areas average to a middle grey is called the "average exposure" method. This works most of the time. The presence of direct light sources in the picture or of large bright or dark areas cause this method to fail.

When a photographer points the meter at the subject and accepts the exposure indicated, he assumes that the bright and dark areas are averaging to a middle grey.

Another way is to determine the exposure for the brightest important area in the picture and for the darkest area where detail must be recorded. The actual exposure used is halfway between these two exposures. This too works most of the time.

Contemporary films have enough latitude to permit any reasonable exposure method to work most of the time. Data-sheet, trial-and-error, averaging and splitting-the-difference all produce usable results. When these methods fail, or when better control is needed, a more precise method is necessary.

Negative quality is mostly controlled by the exposure. Exposure determines correct rendering of dark areas in the subject. It also plays a large part in controlling the size of the grain in the image. Overexposure increases grain size. Correct exposure is determined by correct metering.

For printing from small negatives it is desirable to have a negative which is "thin", i.e., has no more silver than is needed to print detail in the shadows. This is a 'minimum density' negative. It has small grain, and makes a crisp looking print. A minimum density negative can be exposed by pointing the meter at a dark shadowed area of the subject and then making the actual exposure two stops less than the indicated exposure. Remember, the meter is made to read the reflection of a grey card. Because the actual subject is darker, the photographer must correct the indicated exposure and *place* the exposure in the correct tone for correct negative density.

In practice, the darkest area of the subject which must have detail in the print is metered. Since this area (because of the wide angle of the meter's view) will include darker tones, it will correspond to an exposure two *f*-stops less than what would be indicated by a grey card measured in the same light.

Meters built inside cameras have obvious advantages. There are also disadvantages. One is that they are placed so as to meter what the designer feels are important areas of the picture (as seen inside the camera). This takes from the photographer a degree of freedom. At the same time it frees him from routine measurements. This is desirable when he is working with rapidly moving subjects in a changing light environment.

When either telephoto or extreme wide angle lenses are used, the photographer must be cautious about the indicated exposure. For example, a 24-mm lens used indoors will often bring two or more direct light sources into the field of view, bringing the meter indication into error. On the Nikkormat FTN system, for example, the 24-mm lens metering for interiors will be about two stops low because of this. Outdoors, with normal areas averaging, this does not occur.

A telephoto lens makes a built-in meter require interpretation. The narrow view of a telephoto can easily isolate a single texture or color—skin, or grass, or bright clouds. The indicated meter reading must be interpreted since the subject matter differs from a grey card.

EXPOSURE INDEX

Only through trial-and-error testing of a complete system can the photographer learn how to use it in all lighting conditions. With an unevaluated in-camera metering system a safe exposure can usually be achieved by walking up to a dark shadowed area, metering it with the camera, and then exposing two stops less than indicated. Use the meter as though it were a handheld meter. Check this exposure against the exposure suggested by the camera for the total scene.

Any given combination of film, camera, developer and development technique will produce unique results. It is necessary to experiment to determine how a meter, camera and photographer work best together. One of the first experiments should be to determine a System Index—this is the working film speed number to be used for a given type of film.

Cameras are made and assembled on production lines. Small tolerances in manufacturing the mechanical parts and the electrical components may cause the assembled camera system to err in measuring or controlling light. These errors usually cancel. For example, a shutter may be slow and the aperture small. Sometimes tolerances do not cancel but produce definite error. The System Index tests will discover this and permit controlled compensation.

A System Index will help make evenly exposed, minimum density fine grain negatives. These negatives permit enlargements that retain naturalistic rendering of the subject and that have sufficient detail in the shadows to produce good tonal separation. The exact steps for determining a System Index (applying to either handheld or in-camera meters) are outlined later.

THE MATERIALS

The film, chemicals and papers you use for photographic work can be purchased from different sources. These sources often charge different prices. Any given product is more expensive when packaged in small quantities. A ten-sheet package of paper will cost about 30% more per sheet than the same paper in a one-hundred-sheet package.

Generally speaking, the best materials yield the best prints. Cheap paper is usually deficient in silver. The best materials also cost more. The photographic print is essentially a silver suspension, held firmly in a hard gelatin. The more silver there is in the print, the richer the black of the image appears to our eyes. The more silver, the higher the price of the paper.

Use of the best materials should be begun early in your photographic work. Cheaper materials may be used at the very beginning but they will limit your perception, and should be avoided.

FILM

The amount of film you purchase at a time will influence the cost. One hundred sheets of film costs less per sheet than 25 sheets; one hundred feet of 35-mm film in bulk, plus reusable cassettes (Kodak Snap-Caps) cost much less than the equivalent number of preloaded cartridges. Because of general availability of the films and the initial development guides contained in the *Handbook*, the following films are suggested:

FAST FILMS (about ASA 400)

- Tri-X
- HP-4
- Super Hypan

Generally these films are low in contrast and suitable for general work. [N. B. The Kodak company supplies films with the same number or similar names in several sizes of film which are *not* coated with the same emulsion. This creates some confusion, and developing chart information must be examined carefully before processing.]

MEDIUM FILMS (about ASA 125)

- Plus-X Pan
- FP-4
- Versapan
- Verichrome Pan

These films are of medium contrast. Slight changes in development time will cause sharp changes in contrast.

LOW SPEED FILMS (about ASA 32)

- Panatomic-X
- Adox KB 17

These films are subject to rapid increases in contrast with moderate increases in development time.

FILM CHEMICALS

Proprietary formulas or pre-packaged chemicals are most economical for the beginning photographer. Advanced work will require the addition of some chemicals to, or the compounding of, certain formulas.

Mix all chemicals carefully, in the way the manufacturer suggests. Using water that is too hot will cause some degradation of the working agents. In too cold water chemicals are difficult to dissolve. All of the chemicals can be stored in clear bottles but should be stored in the dark because light causes some chemicals, especially developers, to break down rapidly.

Other chemicals may be needed for advanced work. These are listed in appropriate sections of the *Handbook.*

DEVELOPERS	KODAK D-76[1] EDWAL FG-7[2] RODINAL[3] KODAK HC-110[4]
FIXERS[5]	EDWAL QUIK-FIX KODAK RAPID FIXER
HYPO ELIMINATORS[6]	KODAK HYPO CLEARING SOLUTION PERMA WASH (liquid concentrate) GAF QUIK (liquid concentrate)
WETTING AGENTS	EDWAL KWIK WET GAF FLOW 300 KODAK PHOTO-FLO (600)

Notes

1. **D-76** is a prepared powder. Mix it 24 hours before using it. It is diluted to working strength for small films.
2. **Edwal FG-7** is a liquid concentrate. It may be used diluted with water or with a sodium sulfite solution. The sulfite makes a quicker acting developer and one that requires shorter developing times than plain water. Development data for both kinds of dilution are given in the *Handbook.*
3. **Rodinal** is a highly concentrated liquid. It is used in dilutions from 1:25 to 1:100. The very small amounts require careful measurement. A medical syringe is suggested for measuring the developer; a disposable insulin syringe, obtainable from most drugstores, can be used for this purpose.
4. **HC-110** is a syrupy concentrate that may be diluted directly or mixed in a stable intermediate stock solution. Directions are provided on each bottle.
5. **Fixers** listed are sold in liquid torm, with separate hardener solution. Less hardener is used for prints than for film. The mixing instructions are often for solutions of concentrations suitable for commercial processing. These conditions are all right for film but generally are too strong for ordinary processing of prints. Use the chemical concentrate as noted on the manufacturer's package when mixing it for film but note the changes suggested in the *Handbook* under Paper Chemicals.
6. **Hypo Eliminators** are sold as powder or liquid. The powder dissolves easily at working temperature. Each product is similar in that it *does not eliminate* the chemicals used in fixing the print. It simply transforms them into a new chemical state that is easily washed away in the water rinse.

PHOTOGRAPHIC PAPERS

Contemporary enlarging photographic papers are made in three different styles. The newest is the "stabilized print" paper; this has part of the developing agents already in the paper. They are for machine processing but can be processed in tray solutions if need arises. Second is the "variable contrast" papers. These have two emulsions on one base. These emulsions are color sensitive; one is high in contrast, the other low. By using suitable colored filters during printing it is possible to produce prints with varying contrast, yet stock only one kind of paper. The filters are no longer interchangeable—GAF and Kodak each have unique filter systems.

The paper suggested for fine print work is made in numbered contrast grades. The numbers are approximately equivalent in the American system but do not directly compare to the German notation.

KODAK & GAF	CONTRAST	AGFA
1	very low contrast	1
		2
2	normal grade	3
3		4
4	high contrast	5
5		
	very high contrast	6

Kodak makes a grade 0 in their contact print paper (Azo brand).

Any given brand of paper has its own image color, tonal range, and other subtle characteristics that define it. The papers suggested here are all physically smooth, long tonal scale papers that will produce brilliant prints. They will also reveal processing flaws of the negative or the print.

KODAK Medalist (F-1–4) and Kodabromide (F-1–4)
AGFA Brovira (111-1–6)
GAF Jet (GL-1–4)
ILFORD Ilfobrome (IB-0–5)
GAF Cykora (GL 1–4)
AGFA Portrigra Rapid (111-1–4)

The last two papers are "warm tone". The image is brown-black rather than blue-black. The difference in color causes a different sensation of depth in the image. The color of a print paper is altered by the developer used.

Paper is made in two "weights" indicating the stiffness of the supporting paper. Double weight is recommended because it is less easily damaged in processing.

PAPER PROCESSING CHEMICALS

[Some people are allergic to one of the developer's basic chemicals called Metol or Elon. Others easily become sensitized to this chemical. Some of the chemicals used in photography dry the skin and most of the chemicals are irritants to some degree. If dry skin or an allergy is a problem, use rubber gloves. The Playtex Living Glove is best because it is strong, economical, and thin enough to permit handling prints yet retain sensation of textures.]

Four separate solutions are required for the simplest processing of prints. These basic solutions are *Developer, Stop Bath, Fixer,* and *Hypo Eliminator*. Suggested pre-packaged solutions and compounds are:

DEVELOPERS	**KODAK Dektol (may also be compounded as D-72)** **GAF Vividol** **EDWAL Super 111 (sold in small bottles as Platinumtone)**
FIXERS	**See** *Film Chemicals* **for concentrated solutions.**
HYPO ELIMINATORS	**See** *Film Chemicals* **for concentrated solutions.**
STOP BATH	**Glacial Acetic Acid (diluted to 28% stock solution).**

The Fixers are made from the stock solutions used for film processing. Different dilutions are used. The fixing bath can actually etch away some of the silver image if it is too strong, or if the print remains in it too long. The dilutions suggested by the manufacturer are for commercial processing. These are too strong for ordinary processing and the stock should be diluted with 50 per cent more water and the suggested times doubled.

Permanent marking pens can be used to identify all bottles.

OTHER PHOTOGRAPHIC CHEMICALS

It is sometimes desirable to use a solution of selenium to tone the print and intensify it. The toning suggested is quite moderate. The actual process is detailed later. Chemicals needed to tone prints are:

Sodium Thiosulfate (Hypo), 5 pounds
KODAK Rapid Selenium Toner, 1 quart; or the
GAF Flemish Toner, 1 quart.

The balance of chemical compounds in pre-packaged formulas can be altered, and sometimes it is useful to prepare special compounds. The results of prepared formulas are dependable but sometimes other results are desired. Chemicals needed to modify the color or contrast of paper developers are:

Hydroquinone, 4 ounces
Potassium bromide, 1-4 ounces, or the more complex
DUPONT "B-B" Solution, or
KODAK Anti-Fog No. 1

Chemicals needed to prepare special film developers are:

KODAK Elon, 1 pound
Sodium Sulfite, 5 pounds

These are in addition to the paper chemicals noted above. For complete preparation of special developers (See *Comparison of Common Developers*) one also needs:

Sodium Carbonate, 1 pound
Borax, 1 pound

OTHER EQUIPMENT AND MATERIALS

A print must be mounted and viewed before the photographer is finished with it. Sometimes it must be framed or bound under glass. It is necessary to support a print so the mirror-surface of the print will not prevent seeing it.

Finishing materials needed are:

Matt and/or mount board
Matt knife
Straight edge, metal
KODAK Dry Mount Tissue, 150 sheet box
Spotting Brush: WINDSOR & NEWTON Series 7, Size 00
SPOTONE Spotting Dyes

A DEXTER matt cutter is the easiest way to cut a beveled matt. The best mount and matt board is 100% rag. Two brands are available; one from CRESCENT PAPER COMPANY, and the other from BAINBRIDGE PAPER. These boards are expensive. Cheaper boards of reasonable quality are available from Crescent, Strathmore, and Bainbridge. Very cheap boards with dark cores should be used only for test prints.

For cleaning negatives a camels-hair brush is needed. EDWAL Film Cleaner is adequate for cleaning finger marks. Cinema workers use DUPONT Chlorothene, available in large bottles; it is an oil-free cleaner. Negatives may be stored in glassine envelopes or sleeves for temporary storage. The glue used in the seams of these sleeves is hygroscopic and will cause some destruction of the image eventually. A more inert storage envelope is a plastic sleeve available from PRINT FILE, Inc., Box 100, Schenectady, New York 12304. For a more complete understanding of the processes necessary to provide the greatest permanence for prints and negatives, write to the EAST STREET GALLERY, 1408 East Street, Grinnel, Iowa 50112, and purchase the $0.50 booklet on archival processing.

The WESTON INSTRUMENT COMPANY stainless steel thermometer is sturdy but it too can be broken or made inaccurate by careless handling. Temperatures may be accurately measured with the KODAK Color Thermometer.

PRINCIPLES OF PHOTOGRAPHIC WORK

The photographic processes available today will produce usable prints with almost any kind of manipulation. To produce fine prints requires work and care. Controlling your craft rather than allowing it to control you requires patience and some testing of materials.

The successful photographer is an artist and an artisan; he is a visionary and a printmaker. It is a difficult balance to maintain. You will often find yourself leaning one way or the other.

Equipment is expensive. It is well made by commercial standards but it is frail. Never force any threaded fitting. Do not leave electrical equipment operating when it is not needed.

Your own equipment will vary according to your needs and your pocketbook. Equipment must be kept clean and fingerprints removed promptly. Finger oils etch glass. Floors must be kept neat—not merely for appearance—but to prevent contamination from chemicals and damage from dust. After processing any negatives or prints clean the area where you have worked. If chemicals are spilled on the floor, immediately mop them. If you do not they will be tracked into all working areas.

When printing always observe the DRY side and the WET side of a darkroom. The dry side must be kept free of all liquid chemicals. Once packages are opened powdered chemicals should never be stored with paper or film. When moving prints from a wet area, always carry them in a tray so that chemicals will not drip onto the floor.

FILM DEVELOPMENT

Film development controls the quality of the negative. The basic elements of development are time of development, temperature of the developer, and agitation method used. Time must be measured accurately from the first second of immersion into the developer until the second when developer is last draining and the stop bath (or rinse water) is poured on the film.

The development plan is an outline of how the film must be developed to produce a negative which will print in a certain way. The development plan is determined by the nature of the subject before the camera and by the effect desired. In terms of the film itself, increasing development will increase density in the more exposed areas. Increasing development will not help underexposed film.

The development determines how much detail will appear in bright areas of the original subject, as seen in the print, and what the feeling of these tones will be.

Development is controlled by time, temperature, and agitation. Until recently a correct agitation pattern could be produced only with the Kinderman or Nikor stainless steel tanks. For beginners an economical tank is now available in plastic. The PATERSON 5002 single-reel universal tank is available from Braun North-American, Inc., Photo Products Division, 235 Wyman Street, Waltham, Mass. 02154. This tank has an adjustable reel accomodating 35 and 120 film sizes. The flanges of the reel permit adequate developer flow. The lid of the tank seals well enough to permit agitation as described here to be practiced. There is some leakage but no more than with the Nikor tanks. The Kinderman mechanical agitation machine also produces evenly developed negatives but time charts will have to be made by the photographer for using them; do not use the times listed in the *Handbook.* All times shown in the *Handbook* are for the Standard Agitation described below.

The temperature of the developer must be measured in the tank, not in a graduate. The mass of the tank is sufficient to raise or lower the temperature of 16 oz of developer several degrees. The thermometer used must be accurate. Cheap darkroom thermometers are often in error by more than two degrees, and a two degree error (with D-76, for example) equals a full paper contrast grade change error!

CORRECT AGITATION

At the start of the development cycle, lower the film into the tank slowly. It should take 5-10 seconds to place the film in a double tank. A wire 'T' is provided by the manufacturer for this purpose. Place the lid on the tank and immediately invert the tank. Twist it back and forth so the tank is upright again. This causes a rotation about a transverse centerline of the tank.

Invert and re-erect the tank 12 times in each 10 seconds. Agitate continuously this way for the first 30 seconds. At the beginning of each succeeding minute agitate for the first 10 seconds.

This action is not a tossing or spinning of the tank (see Figure 1-2). It is a vigorous reversal of the tank's normal position followed by an immediate return to the correct position. This action causes an interchange of new and old developer but does not encourage any continuing liquid motion. Continuing liquid motion in the tank is responsible for uneven development. Too little agitation is responsible for muddiness in the middle areas of the negative.

A "correct" agitation is one which produces the kind of tones needed to produce a luminous, correctly placed print. Almost any agitation will produce about the same total negative density range (from darkest to lightest). "Correct" agitation will produce clean separation of adjacent tones in the middle of the tonal scale (and in the middle of the strip of film.). Incorrect agitation produces muddy separation of middle tones and density streaks. These are usually along the edge of the negative, about ¼ to ½ inch wide. Sometimes they appear at the end of the film near the center of the loading spiral and are caused by the transverse bars that support the wire flanges.

STANDARD FILM DEVELOPMENT

Suggested normal developing times for medium and high speed films are shown in the STANDARD METHOD DEVELOPMENT TABLE. After a standard method is learned, it can be modified to fit new needs.

Developers are often used in a diluted form. They are mixed first as the manufacturer suggests, and this solution is called a "stock". In practice the stock is then diluted again. The degree of dilution is noted with the developer named first, the dilutent second. For example, D-76 1:1 means one part of stock developer and one part of water. For a small Nikor tank this would mean 7 ounces of D-76 and 7 ounces of water. If the dilution called for was 1:4, this would mean one part of the developer and four parts of water. Using the example of the small Nikor tank again—2¾ ounces of D-76 and 11 ounces of water. The Edwal FG-7 is used 1:15, which means 1 ounce of developer and 15 ounces of water. *The developer is always stated first*, the amount of water used to dilute it second.

STANDARD METHOD DEVELOPMENT (at 70 degrees F).

FILM (and size)	DEVELOPER	DILUTION	DEVELOPMENT TIME	DEVELOPMENT DIRECTIONS
TRI-X				
120	D-76	1:1	8′	Agitate constantly the first 30 seconds, then agitate the first 10 seconds of each minute. Development time starts with the first wetting. Drain time is included in the development time. Dump diluted developers after using them once.
35-mm	D-76	1:1	7½′	
FP-4	D-76	1:1	8′	
PLUS-X				
120	D-76	1:2	10′	
35-mm	D-76	1:4	11′	
VERSAPAN	FG-7	1:15	10′	This is sheet film. In tray development agitation is continuous. The development time is for FG-7 without sulfite.
PLUS-X				
120	FG-7	1:15	10′	Development time is for FG-7 without sulfite.
120	FG-7	1:20	10′	This time and dilution is with 9% sulfite. It is a compensating developer suitable for use in harsh light conditions.
35-mm	FG-7	1:15	8′	

After this point all the films are treated in the same way. Agitation should continue in all solutions.

SOLUTION	TIME	NOTES
Stop Bath	30″	Use a very weak acid solution. One-half ounce of 28% acetic acid stock in a quart of water is enough. Dump after using once.
Fixing Bath	2-5′	Concentrated liquid fixers remove silver rapidly. Do not overfix. Safe fixing is accomplished in twice the time needed to clear the last of the grey emulsion. Throw away the fixer when this time is double clearing time needed for a fresh solution. Powdered Kodak Fixer takes longer.
Rinse	1′	Rinse the film with tap water at 70° F.
Hypo Eliminator	2′	Use according to directions. This does not eliminate but changes the thiosulfate into a compound which washes out easily.
Wash	5′	Fill the tank, agitate several times and dump water. Repeat this ten times.
Wetting Agent	1′	"Wetting" the film with a wetting agent permits the water to flow off smoothly and not leave drops that would mar the image.
Drying	2 hours	Do not dry film in heated cabinets unless necessary. Keep wet film away from all dust. Store dry film as soon as possible.

THE SILVER PRINT

The print is a simplification of tones encountered in the world. The vast range of color and brightness are translated into grey equivalents. The white of the print can never match the sunlit world, nor can the black in the print be as dark as the shadows we see. This translation is both from color to shade and from solid to flat.

The photographic print has the ability to represent tiny variations of grey, evoking a marvelous sense of substance and of texture. Where there are variations of surfaces it is possible to capture variations of tone in the print. Large blank areas of pure white or solid black are also easily realized but these rarely relate to the original surfaces. One definition of the classical fine print is a "full scale—full substance" rendering. This print displays tones from solid black through to pure white in the same way the subject is seen to range from black shadows to glistening highlights. This print also records the sensation of substance—its mass and weight—in the object photographed. Full scale—dark to light; full substance—the sense of the original mass. Tonal scale controls the sensation of *surface* of the subject which one feels on viewing the fine print.

A print with a sense of internal light, which seems able to stand by itself, not depending on special surroundings, may be called a *fine print.* This sense of light does not exist in reproduction. Such a definition is subjective; it is dependent in part on the experiencing of fine prints. One cannot learn what to look for in a print by examining only reproductions in books and magazines. Original prints must be sought out and studied.

The reproduced print is a source of information about the photograph but is not the original photograph. It is always different, sometimes stronger! Learn to evaluate both print and copy. Each has its own character, its own visual values. Seek out fine prints and learn by the direct experiencing. Study reproductions to learn more about other kinds of photographic seeing.

PREPARATION FOR PRINTING

The whole point of the technical discipline is to produce a method of working that frees the photographer to concentrate on the image, not on the mechanics of photography.

Chemicals should be mixed as suggested on the packages. There are other ways to mix them but the suggested ways will produce dependable results. Developers should be carefully prepared ahead of time so the chemicals are thoroughly dissolved. Sulfite, especially, often appears to mix easily and yet requires time to fully dissolve.

Trays should be washed both before and after using them. This double action prevents contamination. Film reels must be washed, not merely rinsed off. The wetting agent often leaves a film which makes it difficult to reload the reels.

PRINTING INSTRUCTIONS

Prepare the following trays:

Developer: Dektol, Vividol, Dilute 1:2 for Kodak or GAF papers; 1:3 for Brovira. **The standard developing time is three minutes.** Use the developers at 70 degrees, or slightly above. Part of the developer weakens rapidly below 70 degrees.

The print must be immersed smoothly, with a single stroke. Insert it into the developer face up (to prevent bubbles from forming). Developing time affects contrast of the image. Minimum time is about one minute. Maximum time is about five minutes. Experiment alone will show how long your safelight conditions will permit you to develop the print.

Agitate constantly. Lift the print, drain it for 2-3 seconds, and lay it back into the developer. Agitation will affect the separation of tones. Some contrast control is also available through changing the concentration of the developer. Stock developer will produce greater contrast. Developer can be diluted as much as 1:4 for softer results.

Do not over-use the developer. A rule of thumb is that each ounce of developer stock is good for one 8×10 print, when fine work is attempted. Start with eight ounces of developer and 24 ounces of water in an 8×10 tray. This solution is good for about 10 fine prints before dumping.

Stop Bath: Time in the stop bath is 20 seconds. Use two ounces of a 28% acetic acid solution in two quarts of water. Drain the print over the developer for 3-5 seconds and then slide it into the stop bath. Agitate, drain, and lay it in the Fixing Bath.

Fixing Bath: Time is always the minimum suggested by the manufacturer, when usingfresh stock. Do not over-fix prints. Silver will be etched away if minimum safe silver removal times are exceeded by more than two minutes.

Good initial agitation will prevent chemical stains. After one minute of agitation of the print in the Fixer it may be examined under white light. After studying the print return it to the Fixer for the balance of the recommended time. Keep track of the number of prints used in a gallon of solution. Each gallon is good for about 120 prints.

Interim Storage: If print washing facilities are separate from the immediate processing area, store prints in a tray with running water, or in a tray of water which is changed occasionally. This will prevent etching away of silver by the fixing salts.

Hypo Eliminating Solution: Time is always the minimum or suggested times provided by the manufacturer. Prepare a gallon of working-strength solution from one of the concentrated stocks listed. This gallon of working solution will be good for about 120 8×10 prints, provided they have been given a short wash before treatment. Agitate the prints constantly in the hypo eliminating solution.

Final Wash: Time in final wash is 20 minutes for regular prints, one hour for archival. If a tray with a Kodak Print Wash Siphon is used for washing prints, never wash more than 10 prints at a time. Store the excess prints in a tray of water until they can be safely washed. Agitate the prints manually if necessary.

Drying: Drain the prints until all free water is removed. If you wish to squeegee the surface, keep a special sponge or the Kodak bar squeegee. Dry the prints on nylon-screening drying racks and then flatten them in a dry-mounting press. Do not use rotary drum dryers unless no other dryer is available. Prints may be dried on towels, at home, with safey. Lay the print face up until all surface water has gone and then turn it over until it is dry to the touch. This will prevent any marks appearing in the gelatin.

BASIC PRINTING

Prepare a clean working area. Put out only materials you will need. These include photographic paper, developer, fixer, acid, negatives, a negative brush, a clean piece of paper to focus the image on, and possibly an enlarging focusing magnifier.

The actual sequence of printing is almost always the same: a contact proof, test strip, enlarged proof, and finally a try at a finished print. The test strip can often be avoided by comparing exposures on the proof sheet.

The contact proof is the first step. Raise the lamphouse of the enlarger until it illuminates a rectangle or square on the enlarger baseboard a little larger than 8×10 inches.

Examine your enlarger lens. Learn what the maximum aperture is. Learn to count the f numbers down from that aperture, so that you can set the lens to any given aperture without having to strain to see the marking on the lens.

Close the lens to *f*-16. Use a contact print frame or a piece of clear heavy glass to hold the negatives and paper in intimate contact. Place the paper emulsion up, the negative emulsion down, and the glass on top.

Expose through the negative, using the enlarger as a light source. Cover half the paper with a piece of cardboard and expose for five seconds. Uncover the paper and expose another five seconds. One half now has five seconds and the other half ten seconds exposure. Develop the print for three minutes. As it develops watch what is happening. The image should first appear at about 20-30 seconds of development. After 1½ minutes it should appear complete. The last 1½ minutes of development should darken only the shadow areas of the image.

Fix the print. Drain it over the developer, put it into the stop bath, and then after 20 seconds into the fixing bath. Agitate for one minute. Rinse the fixer off the print with water and take it into white light and examine it. Decide which exposure was better—the dark or the light one. If one seems too dark and the other too light, plan on making the next exposure halfway between.

The test strip and the trial print are generally both necessary steps in printmaking. The test strip is a piece of photographic paper two inches wide by the length of the sheet of paper.

The test strip: Expose across the image area (in a projection print) so that important light and dark places in the image are exposed. Expose in sections. Cover all but a fourth of it. Expose for five seconds. Uncover half. Expose another five seconds. Uncover three-fourths and expose another five seconds. Uncover all of it and expose for a last five seconds. Develop the print. If the correct *f*-number was used the exposures will "bracket" the desired density.

Most contemporary enlargers have similar printing characteristics. A properly exposed and developed negative will produce a usable print on a "normal" contrast grade of paper if exposed at f-16 for 10 to 20 seconds.

Examine the test strip both for correct exposure and for correct contrast. The print should have small solid black areas and equally small white areas. It should not have larger black and white solid areas. These mean the contrast is too high.

Time and materials can be saved by "bracketing" an unknown condition. If the exposure produces a print that seems light, make a print too dark. If the test print seems low in contrast, i.e., "flat", make a print that is too contrasty. Try to "cross-over" to the opposite condition in one step. This is preferable to "creeping up" to a solution. We lie to ourselves when we do this because our eyes tire easily.

INTRODUCTION TO ZONE TERMINOLOGY

"Zones" are names given by Ansel Adams to parts of the grey scale. The "Zone" is also a verbal tool. The term was first used by Adams; it is fundamental to his disciplined system of controlling the negative and the print (see the Basic Photo Series, Morgan and Morgan, Hastings-on-the-Hudson, New York).

The Zone System can be used to describe the tones of a photographic print. The photographic grey scale does not have equally separated steps of grey corresponding to equal intervals of exposure. The first four equal exposure steps above black are very dark tones—black to very dark grey. The next three equal increases of exposure are well separated grey tones. The last three steps of exposure make tones that are nearly white.

The best black the paper can produce is called Zone 0. The least change from this that can be seen is Zone I. Zone II is nearly black. Zone III is very dark. Zone IV is the beginning of the middle tones, and it is a dark, rich grey.

Zone IV is the start of the most useful part of the grey scale. One can make a print that contains only the middle tones (Zones IV-VII) and it will be a passable picture. This is what most "drugstore" prints are like.

Zones IV, V, VI, and VII are dark grey, middle grey, light grey, and pale grey, respectively. They are well separated tones; they differ one from the other by only one interval of exposure, by one *f*-stop increase.

Zones VII, VIII, and IX are pale grey, almost white, and white, respectively. Like the dark tones at the other end of the scale, they are close and difficult to compare or to separate without experience.

ZONES 0-III are almost black

ZONES IV-VII are middle tones, well separated, and contain most of the information about textures and shapes.

ZONES VII-IX are light, and close.

CORRECT PRINT EXPOSURE

The correct exposure for the print is determined by the light areas (Zones VII-IX). Examine the test print. If all areas are too dark, stop the lens down. Do not decrease printing time below 10 seconds. Most mechanical timers are erratic for intervals less than 10 seconds. Longer printing times also allow time for local controls to be used with repeatable accuracy. A correctly exposed and developed negative can be printed correctly with one or two test strips. If the negative has been improperly developed special work may be needed.

CHOOSING THE CORRECT CONTRAST GRADE OF PAPER

Examine the test strip for correct rendering of the dark Zones (0-III). *The exposure of the print is determined by the high Zones; the correct contrast grade of paper is determined by the low Zones (the black and near-black areas).*

If the print appears to be right—have detail in the highlights; detailed but near-black shadows—continue working. Make an enlarged full-frame print.

When the shadows are not dark enough, use the next higher paper contrast grade. Make a new test strip. Fix it and then examine for correct shadows.

It is possible that the dark areas of the print may merge. If they appear as a solid black use a lower contrast grade and the tones will separate.

MAKING AND USING THE TRIAL PRINT

There are several steps to making a fine print. First there is a contact print, a study proof. This yields basic information about the possibilities of the negative. Then there is an enlarged proof. Between this and the fine print may be one, or several, intermediate prints.

Make a full-frame print. Use the exposure and contrast information gained from the test strips. This print should be "straight", no attempts at local correction. Fix the print and examine it in white light. Study it for overall accuracy of the exposure; the correctness of the contrast grade; areas that may need special work.

Ask yourself: *Should the whole negative be used for the print? What portion of it will make the best picture?*

Look at the print again. Try to see it as work done by someone else. Look for the sense of the surfaces in the photograph, the rendering of textures and volumes, of transparency, and mass.

The print must be satisfactory on at least two levels: as a translation of reality to a print, and as shapes on the surface of a piece of paper. The subject of the print is the shapes and tones in the print, regardless of what these shapes are supposed to represent.

If the print seems too dark reduce the exposure about 50%. If it is too light increase the exposure the same amount. If the contrast seems too high reduce the contrast grade. Sometimes a full paper grade is too much change. When this happens modify the developer instead of changing paper grades.

Decide what local manipulations are needed. Edge burning is often necessary to "bring in" the print toward the center; the eye is drawn inward by the dark edges. Some areas of the print may be rendered "correctly", yet need to be changed when seen as a part of the whole print.

The trial print will yield information needed to produce a fine print. The fine print is an *excellent* print in terms of printmaking and also it is the best rendering of the photographer's vision.

Make another print incorporating the planned changes. Assuming that the corrections made to this point are right, it is difficult to be certain of further changes until the print is dry. *Tonal separations change and darken as the print dries.* The amount of change varies from one kind of paper to another. Dry the print. Study it before attempting a final statement.

Note exposures, *f*-numbers and special problems on the back of the work print. A soft lead pencil is good for this; do not press hard. Excess pressure will cause marks on the surface of the print.

CONTRAST CONTROL THROUGH DEVELOPER DILUTION

The developer dilution suggested for Brovira was 1:3. This dilution produces a soft-working developer, suitable for the slightly higher-than-normal contrast inherent in the Brovira No.3 paper. Most developers can be used "straight" or diluted as much as 1:4. Many paper developers will produce somewhat browner tones as dilution is increased because of the change in concentration of the Hydroquinone, relative to the Elon.

THE FINISHED PRINT

The finished print grows from an understanding of the possibilities of the photograph.

After you have "lived with" a print for a time, try making a finished print. It is difficult to make a final version of a photograph immediately after making a trial print. We usually see only one aspect of a picture at a time—the subject, the printing or the graphics of the print. With time we come to understand all the parts and how to bring them into harmony.

Making a finished fine print differs from making a trial print. The developer is used more conservatively so that the richest tones can be produced. Manipulations are made both with greater freedom and with greater understanding. The result is a new photograph.

If chemical modifications of the developer are used, add them just before use. Developer formulations are stable as manufactured, changing them makes them unstable. Modified developers decompose rapidly. Develop no more than one 8×10 inch print in each ounce of developer stock. If you are leaving the darkroom for more than a few minutes cover the developer with another tray to reduce oxidation.

The first test print may be harsh because the developer is fresh. Even here it is desirable to "bracket"—make prints a little darker and a little lighter than what you think is right. Do this until you have enough experience to predict accurately changes when the print dries.

Ansel Adams and Minor White both discuss *previsualizing* the print. For Adams, this term is associated with the physical tones of the print, the translation of subject brightnesses into print equivalents. For White, the term includes this technical meaning but has been extended to incorporate possible associations of the image. Previsualization in either sense is possible if controls are applied.

Contemporary photographic esthetics includes both previsualization and postvisualization. This means seeing image possibilities after the negative has been made. It is not an excuse for poor previsualization or bad technique: it is a supplement to working only with the camera. Postvisualization can be simple printing with more or less contrast, or complicated multiple printing, sandwiching negatives, or making non-silver prints by one of the processes outlined later in the *Handbook*.

In summation, make an exposure for the correct rendering of the highlight areas of the subject. Develop the print. Examine the shadows. Decide if they are too dark, too light, or correct. On the basis of this evaluation decide what contrast grade of paper is correct, or what developer concentration must be used.

1. Expose and develop for correct highlights.
2. Examine the print for correct shadows.
3. Change contrast of paper or developer concentration to make shadows print correctly.
4. If this is impossible, remake the negative. Only a correct negative will yield a right print.

THE PHOTOGRAPHIC CYCLE

1.	**Vision**	Discovering the possible photographic subject.
2.	**Craft, supporting vision**	Preparing to make a photograph: locate the subject in the groundglass or the viewfinder. Calculate the exposure and prepare the development plan. Re-see the subject and make the exposure.
3.	**Craft**	Develop the film according to the development plan.
4.	**Revision: or proof of previsualization**	In the darkroom look on the projected negative as a new photographic subject. Experience it freshly. Compare initial responses to the subject in this new image.
5.	**Craft-Vision-Craft**	Make a print. Study it and then decide if the initial vision was fulfilled, or if new print possibilities can be discovered. Explore the possibilities of postvisualization. Then attempt to make a finished print.
6.	**Craft-Vision**	Mount and finish the image. Do not do this automatically but responsively.
7.	**Criticism**	This is a creative act: discovering the contents of the image and it's quality.

(upper photo) Students at Ohio University explore possible image associations by using potter's clay, which permits a non-verbal investigation of the photograph. (lower photo) example of photograph and clay interpretation.

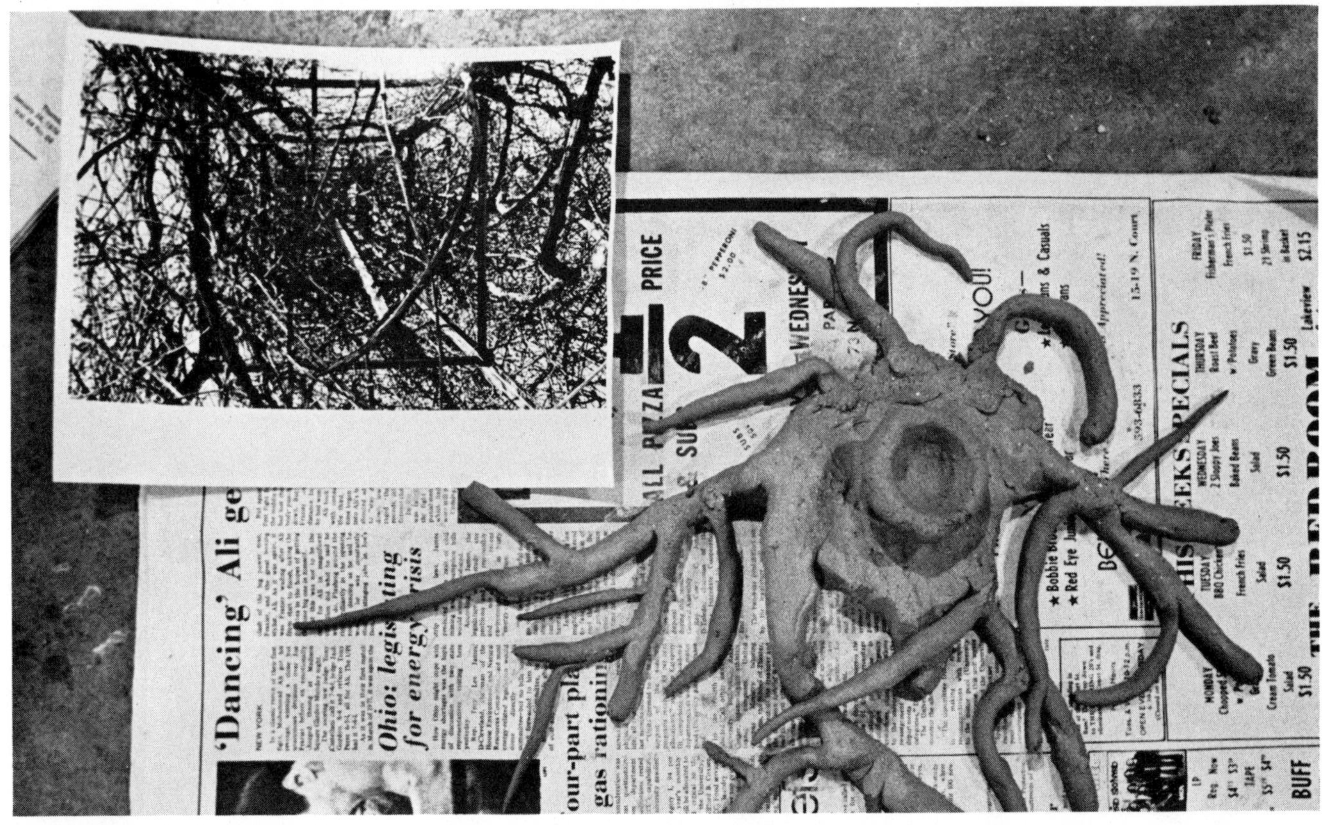

photographs by John Carson Graves

2: response & critique

Mastering the medium of photography requires controlling the craft and understanding the meaning of the image. To improve your photograph means to discover and understand what you photograph, and what you reveal through the print. First, understand what happens when the subject in front of the camera is translated through the mechanism of lens and film into an image. Second, discover what happens when the print is viewed, by yourself and by someone else.

Attempt to see what the camera sees. Attempt to discover what you see when you view the print. Attempt to discover what others see when they look at your print.

Work of this kind cannot be done only on craftsmanship or only on understanding. Work cannot be done on one area of mastery and not on another. For example, pointing the camera is an act of selection. Selections are based on both conscious and unconscious reasons. Some simple reasons we choose a certain point of view are the shapes we see please us; the tones are attractive; a story is associated with the subject. We may believe the image will tell that story.

The photographic print can become a new subject, suitable for study. It may create an illusion of actions seen by the camera. It may be the shapes of the print that interest us, or the tones which please us; these and the illusions of reality may evoke a story that can be paraphrased in words.

Discover what your camera sees. Then discover the image you have made with it. These discoveries become tools, to be carried along the next time you photograph.

A first step to understanding is to know how your camera changes things; the next is understanding what you do when you encounter the print. When understanding is reached, then evaluation or judgement may be made, if it is necessary.

Experience tempered with frequent exercise in making judgements separates the beginner from the advanced worker far more than sophistication in the use of the materials and mechanics of photography. It is the difference between the artist and the skilled technician. One is capable of evaluating the esthetic product, the other of the polish of the performance.

The advanced photographer has more experience with materials and equipment than the beginner; he has more experience in understanding the making of the photograph and then judging it when that is necessary. He brings greater resources to a judgement. These resources are books read, paintings, prints and films seen, and general life experience. The mature photographer has learned to judge his own work, eliminating craftsmanship faults and reinforcing his personal statement.

MAKE A TRIAL DEFINITION OF 'PHOTOGRAPH'

The photograph may refer to an illusionistic presentation of an action or an event. This illusion is usually a story telling event. Or the photograph may refer to an isolated object, or set of things. This 'documents' the existence of that object. Such an image also has some story telling properties. The image may be important because it is itself; the patterns, tones and shapes somehow have meaning in themselves.

The photograph you make will reflect your own needs and interests. The artist Paul Klee wrote that "I and the picture look each other in the face." The photographer Frederick Sommers said that "art is images you carry. You cannot carry nature with you, but you carry images of nature. When you go out to make a picture you find you are moved by something which is in agreement with an image you held already within yourself."

Criticism of the photograph can be directed at the print or at the process of making the photograph. The first is concerned with *what* you photograph, and the relationships between you, the subject, photograph and possibly even the viewer. The second is concerned with how well the print is made; of course this criticism reflects current standards of print quality and styles of printing.

If your concern with the photograph is in terms of the quality of the technical accuracy of the rendering, then a certain set of tests and comparisons can be made. If your concern is for an effect of the image, another series of examinations are possible.

When the photograph is being examined for its value as a record, accuracy controls the judgement. Skin areas must resemble skin; clouds look like clouds; trees have roundness and look like trees. Craft problems limit value. Underexposure makes shadows black and overdevelopment creates harsh and featureless highlights. Craft failures lead to failures of the illusion.

DISCOVER THE IMAGE YOU HAVE MADE

Each photographer believes his images are fairly clear, that another person ought to be able to see what he sees in the picture. His idea of the photograph is often not the only possible idea.

This is not to say he must know his intention before making the exposure. Often we photograph in order to discover why we see, what somehow is important. In this case we do not know what we have seen until we discover it in the negative, or the print.

TRY TO DEFINE 'PHOTOGRAPHY'

Photography may be an act of recording surfaces, textures, event. Or it may be a tool used to assist the printmaker. It provides a special kind of tonal scale, image color and illusionistic possibility.

The photographic creative act may take place all at once, just before the shutter is released (and all the rest be mechanical work yielding a proof of that creation). Or it may be a series of steps, with other creative solutions possible at the end of each step. In this case the first print may well be clumsy and inept. This does not matter because it is possible to take the discovered vision back to the process and rework it. Rework is common in most forms of printmaking Inspiration is assisted by logic and experience to form a new object, the print. Yvor Winters affirmed this when he wrote that "unpremeditated art is usually bad."

The act of printing can be a discovery of vision. This vision can be carried back into the process of photography. The process may yield an illusionistic image or a print which has value as an object.

Three questions have been posed: try to define 'photograph'; discover the image you have made; try to define 'photography'. These have value only if they are answered in terms of your own needs.

Working answers to these questions are possible through investigation. Craftsmanship evaluations are straightforward if the purpose of the picture is understood.

Craftsmanship can be evaluated without involving anyone else at first. After doing this, make a study of the shapes and tones of the image. Then discover the essential gesture of the image. Finally, the possible verbal paraphrases of it can be discovered.

Eventually, others' responses to the image must be sought and weighed.

Start by looking at your print. See how well it is crafted. This is different than looking at the 'subject' revealed in the print. Understanding the accomplishments of craft becomes the first problem. This can be assisted by comparing the image to a set of standards.

FIRST COMPARISON: Your print to a standard photographic print.

Choose a photograph you wish to use as a standard. This is simply what you think is an excellent print, and one which relates to your work. This must be an appropriate standard. Use a real print, not a memory of an ideal print.

The standard you use will change with experience. Most beginners choose prints with high contrast; the superficial vigor of large black areas appeals to them. As experience is gained with high contrast simplifications they seem less exciting. A richer tonal scale becomes desired. A change of taste requires a new comparison image.

Your comparisons should yield affirmations. It is easy to comment destructively. It is hard work to make a comparison and affirm creative possibilities, yet at the same time recognize craft problems and seek their solutions. Affirmations will help provide energy to work out solutions. Even advanced photographers have difficulty with the materials. Unwillingness to recognize and analyze problems will merely inhibit growth.

When choosing a standard choose a suitable image. Comparisons with unsuitable standards are misleading. Experimental work cannot logically be compared to a 'straight' print, for example.

Some terms of craft comparison are:

- image color
- clarity of whites
- richness of blacks
- liveliness of intermediate grey tones
- evenness of tone (agitation and development)
- suitability of grain for image
- absence of mechanical blemishes
- suitability of paper surface, contrast grade and color
- adequacy of mounting and finishing

Study your print. Compare it with the standard print; compare it with maximum black and maximum white patches from the same kind of paper. Compare the darkest places in the print to the black patch, and the small pure highlight whites with the white patch.

Decide what is the purpose of the print. A fine print will be judged by different standards than a print for newspaper reproduction. A fine print may use the whole scale of the paper; the reproduction print will look somewhat grey and flat, yet be the *proper* print for the purpose.

SECOND COMPARISON: Your idea of the photograph to the print you have made.

This study is possible to approach verbally and through graphical analysis. Meanings possible in the photograph are compounded by the associations we bring to them from our general experiences. First, limit your study to the graphic meanings.

Place a sheet of clean tracing paper over the photograph. Draw the borders of the print. Carefully outline each light area of the picture—the tones from light grey through to white. Mark this sheet "high values".

Replace this sheet with a clean piece of tracing paper. Draw the borders again, then outline all the middle grey areas. Sometimes a tone will be difficult to place; you will have to decide whether it is a middle or a light grey. Mark this sheet "middle tones".

On a third sheet outline all the dark-grey to black areas.

On each sheet, using a soft drawing pencil, shade in solid tones all the areas within the closed contours. Do this carefully. Each tracing becomes a new visual statement.

Pin up the tracings. Study them. Look at each one. Study the patterns made. These can be interesting, dull, even, lopsided, scattered, clumped.

The character of the tracing will help disclose the composition of the picture, and the real subject of it. Photographers make pictures of *patterns of light* and they photograph *things.* The objects in front of the camera and the patterns coexist. Sometimes the pattern of light dominates the image, making its own statement; the pattern may support the illusion of the thing before the lens, or distract from it and make its own statement. The tracings will help to reveal what the real subject of the photograph is in fact.

Examine the tracings. Compare each in turn with the original print. Decide which pattern is dominant, i.e., which seems to carry the spirit of the image. Put the others away with the photograph. From the dominant tracing try to draw the essential gesture of the image. This relates to the *gestalt* of the print. Paul Klee called the gestalt the "living being" of the image in contrast to the mere form of it.

The gesture of this spirit may be a moving line, a shape, an arrow, an expanding field. It may be heavy, light, closing, or opening. The drawing of the gestalt is a nonverbal paraphrase of the photograph.

Compare this drawing with the original print. See if they do in fact relate. If there is a difference of spirit there may have been mistakes made in tracing, or in choosing the dominant pattern. Perhaps the photograph you made was not what you had thought. There is a feeling of confusion when the drawing of the gesture seems to disagree with the image. Sometimes the analysis is rejected. Ask "what did I intend?" Then ask "what did I produce?" Sometimes one is unable to answer these questions immediately.

Meanings within an image are sometimes hard to discover. Compare the image you had intended to the image produced. The tracing will help disclose the component parts.

Use of the verbal associations triggered by an image can help reveal meanings. These must come from the photograph. For example, take several photographs and write the purpose of each picture on a file card. Put the prints and the cards away in separate places. After several days examine the prints again. Look at each picture, and on a new card write all possible reasons for the image. Try to see it as a stranger would see it.

Examine each photograph and make notes. When finished, compare the file cards for each photograph. The response written one day and possibilities seen on another day are often not identical. The differences may help you discover some meanings not seen at first.

Often a photographer thinks the subject is one thing and the tracings and questions reveal important secondary meanings. The questions and the answers become additions to your tools for discovery. They can permit more skillful creation of photographs, after learning to accept and use them.

THIRD COMPARISON: The photograph you see to the photograph someone else sees.

Learn the difference between private vision and public consensus on the meaning of that vision. This can be done easily in a class or where a trusted and responsive audience is available.

You see possibilities of a picture in the original subject when you make a photograph and you see certain meanings in the print. You derive pleasure from the image. When another person looks at your photograph he may feel something similar or he may see something very much different. He brings his own experience to the image.

The photographic image will have a different meaning for each viewer. Most interpretations of a strong image will fall into a limited range of statements. But some images will have radically different meanings for people with different backgrounds, especially if they are not guided in their discovery by means of a title.

The clarity of your statement is variable. Hardly any artist is willing to believe this until he has rude encounters with his audience.

Perform an experiment to show how easily meaning can change. Take any four photographs. Place them in line on the wall. Study them. Discover where they interact, and how they work together. Interchange the first and third print. Look at the new set made by this change. Discover what happens to the meaning of the set. Now interchange the second and third prints. Look at the new combinations and discover what feelings it produces. Finally interchange the first and last print, and examine the result. Each set of images will have different visual meanings (some dull, some more exciting).

If the simple changing of the order of the prints changes meaning, then how much more seeing them through different eyes will change meaning! Each person sees his own image. This can be investigated where a group of photographers can work together. Exchange prints; each photographer offers and receives two prints. Take your two and make a catalogue of the contents. Note the *objects*, *shapes* and *associations* which these evoke.

Define *objects* as things which were before the lens of the camera; *shapes* as forms found in the print; *associations* as the feelings, thoughts and possibilities of meaning which arise as you experience the print.

Take note of all of these. Decide how strong each response is.

This investigation should be brief. Keep it simple. Direct your attention to the print. It is easy to stray into private fantasies. You will uncover some of your own attitudes while doing this, about what photography ought to be, what prints ought to look like, and so on. Discover the range possible. Do not try to deny its existence.

When you have finished with your prints, meet as a group. Each person can read what he has written, and explain it if necessary. Many people are uneasy when talking about photographs. They feel they do not have an adequate vocabulary. They simply do not trust their own responses. They feel that being honest and telling what they feel means they are being "critical", i.e., being destructive. This kind of investigation is not inherently destructive but affirmative. You are finding out what is possible, not taking anything away.

A variation of this is to supply one photograph of your own and one taken from a magazine. Choose a picture you feel is interesting. Because the magazine photographs are not by you or your friends you may be less protective, and more free to respond.

Go a step further. Seek the responses of people who are not photographers. Photographers have certain responses to print quality, subject matter, or even how currently popular the subject of the picture is in the competitive work being published.

Before you ask others about your photographs, decide what you wish to learn. Are you concerned with what people see in general when they look at a photograph, or what their response is to your special interests?

Take three photographs to work with. You may wish to include one which is not yours but which you have already catalogued. Ask fifteen persons to look at the prints. Find people who have time to look and who are in a relatively quiet place. Ask each person the same question: "what do you see in the picture?" This is different than asking what is seen in the print, or the photograph. The words used are important. Whatever you ask will in some way limit the answer.

The person you are interviewing must believe in your interest. Your attitude, the way you listen and the way you present the prints will all influence him. Take notes openly. Discover the person's background and attempt to discover how background relates to response.

When the person runs out of words ask: "is that all you see?" Do not be more directive. Gain general information but do not pursue specific goals. Watch the person's face: nonverbal communication is important in these interviews.

When you have completed one set of interviews, study your results. Does background affect response in any way you can discover. How many people saw something in the photograph similar to what you deemed important? How many people discovered other aspects of the image which were more important to them? How many people looked at the subject, how many saw the print as a print, and what was the general tone of the emotional response? Other questions may arise from studying your notes.

After the first try, specific questions have value. If the technique works for you, take these or other pictures and talk to new people. The next time ask specific questions, for example, "what relationships do you see between *this* and *that* in the picture?"

In general, people see a photograph as a magic window through which they can reach out and touch the object on the other side. Or they see it as a pattern of shapes, tones and simulated textures. One person, in other words, deals with the subject of the photograph and the other with graphics. A person may respond both ways at once but one or the other will dominate. Either type of person will probably also respond to his imaginings which are triggered by seeing the print.

A viewer will see the print and his fantasy about it at the same time. Your problem is to relate the answers given you to your photograph and to your vision.

Try to carry this information back into your work with the camera. The following exercise is a way to do this consciously. Two photographers work together. One is a leader, the other the photographer. After an exposure is made, they change roles.

Having found a place to work, the photographer blindfolds himself. The leader takes him to the place the photographer describes. The camera is handled by the photographer but the leader verifies each step. Let the photographer estimate the exposure and attempt to make the settings on the camera, place it, focus it, and do all the mechanical work by himself. The leader verifies it as being right or wrong.

Meanwhile the photographer describes the scene he thinks he is photographing. The leader tells him to move left, right, etc., to produce the scene. But the leader asks no questions of his own. When everything is in order, and both parties believe they are making the same photograph, make an exposure. The photographer removes his blindfold and examines the scene on the groundglass or through the viewfinder.

Now, compare the mental image of the photograph, the groundglass image and the image the leader has seen. Let the leader describe what the effect of the image was on him. Exchange roles and repeat the work.

While working through these exercises and experiments you will make three kinds of comparisons:

1. Your print to a standard print.
2. Your idea of the photograph to the print you have made.
3. The photograph you see to the photograph someone else sees.

The print will always reflect yourself. Discovering how this reflection looks to others is difficult but necessary work.

CLASSIFICATION AND JUDGEMENT

There is a difference between the above kind of understanding of an image and making a judgement of a photograph. Understanding is the result of response, experience and investigation. A judgement uses this investigation and moves on to attempt to assign value to the work.

Judgement often is necessary, though not always. We can "like" or fail to like a print. But if we need to make a judgement then understanding is necessary.

All the work described so far has been essentially reflexive. It has turned the photographer back on to himself, to apply the results of his understanding as best he can to the making of new photographs. But your photograph will not always be judged relative to your possibilities. There will come a time when it is evaluated by comparing it to existing photographs.

Sometimes it is impossible for a photographer to judge his own work. But one can try to make a judgement. To do this it is necessary to discover the current standards of quality, why they exist, how they have changed and what they imply. Know this, add it to your understanding and your response, and you are prepared to make a judgement of where a photograph stands in contemporary photography.

The question of value is raised when one attempts to make a judgement. You may value a print uncritically because it moves you, because you feel like saying "I like it." This is the way we usually choose prints to live with, to hang upon our walls.

Whether you need to raise the question of judgement at all depends on the way you are using photography. If photography is a means to psychological self-exploration, then esthetic judgement may be unimportant. However, once a photograph is published a judgement will follow.

Judging requires language appropriate to the photograph at hand. Just as an inappropriate standard image will lead to confusion in judging craft, so inaccurate language prohibits accurate judgement. The image must be identified in a general way, i.e., placed in a category. A critic in the *Village Voice* recently referred to the "dialects of the language of photography" and then spoke of young photographers who consistently speak "the language of Robert Frank". Such an analogy is useful.

Classification of an image precedes judgement. Inappropriate images cannot be competitively evaluated. Classifications are necessary, and classification is difficult. If the classification is not appropriate the judgement may be bad or useless.

One may classify the image on the basis of the general type of picture it is (or the *genre*). Or it may be classified according to the *function* to which the picture has been put in its lifetime. Or on the basis of the *technical problems* associated with its making. Many different classifications have been given to photographic images by critics and historians, for example: *social landscape, lyrical, documentary, straight print, photojournalist, manipulated,* and so on. Each classification system has inherent problems.

When you encounter a system of classification, try to see what it is based on. Terms relating to image *functions* include:

documentary: when the accuracy of the recording power of the camera seems to be most important.
pictorial: when the handsomeness of the picture itself dominates.
graphic: when the shapes of tones on the print are most valued.
equivalent: when the image works strongly for many viewers as a metaphor.

These terms describe the way the image is used. Pictures often fall in more than one category.

Because photography is so involved with the mechanics of making the print, *technical means* have been used for the basis of some classifications. Terms encountered include:

cameras: the effect small cameras and large format cameras have on the image.
films: the possibilities and problems with small film, very fast film, fine grain film, etc.
contrast: use of high contrast, conversions from continuous to halftone images, low key, high key, etc.
prints: color prints, warm tone and cold tone papers, textured and smooth surfaces, whiteness of paper stock, etc.

The terms of such a system refer to mechanical problems.

Sometimes a classification system centers on the subject of the photograph, the thing in front of the camera. These photographic *genres* include:

landscape: the natural landscape, principally unmodified by man's working.
cityscape: the city with or without people in interaction.
figure: the naked human shape.
portrait: as psychological record or public document.
snapshot: the private response to a moment, a mnemonic.
scientific record: the accurate catalogue of detail.

Other terms come to mind which fit this kind of classification. A recent addition is that of the *social landscape* where the subject is the person interacting with the environment.

All these systems of classification overlap. Make any system you use as clear as possible; and understand the underlying structure. In grade school one is taught not to add apples and oranges; in the same way be cautious, when evaluating photographs, to consider the kind of image actually at hand. When responding to a photograph feel it as fully as you can; when judging it know the standards applicable.

You may like or dislike a photograph without understanding. To extend Klee's idea that the artist makes an image that is a mirror of himself—we respond to images that mirror ourselves. Sometimes the response takes the form of hostility, sometimes of liking. It is not possible to evaluate a published image without making a critical judgement. This is a delicate balancing of comparisons. Critical judgement requires personal response, plus a knowledge of the standards of the medium.

Feel an esthetic response, then analyze the photograph. Learn the history of the photograph and of the photographer, study the art of its time; against all this place your own reaction.

The steps to a critical judgement are:

know the biographical or historical background of the work.
know the theories that supported the work in its own time.
understand the meaning of the work in terms of the art of its time.
discover the methods used to create its effects.
balance your response against a summary of the above.

The quality of your judgement depends on your knowledge of the medium. The validity of your judgement depends on the thoroughness of your investigation and the sensitivity you bring to the photograph.

The change from a beginning photographer to a mature photographer is not only a result of increased technical competence. It is also a result of increased critical awareness of ourselves and of our images.

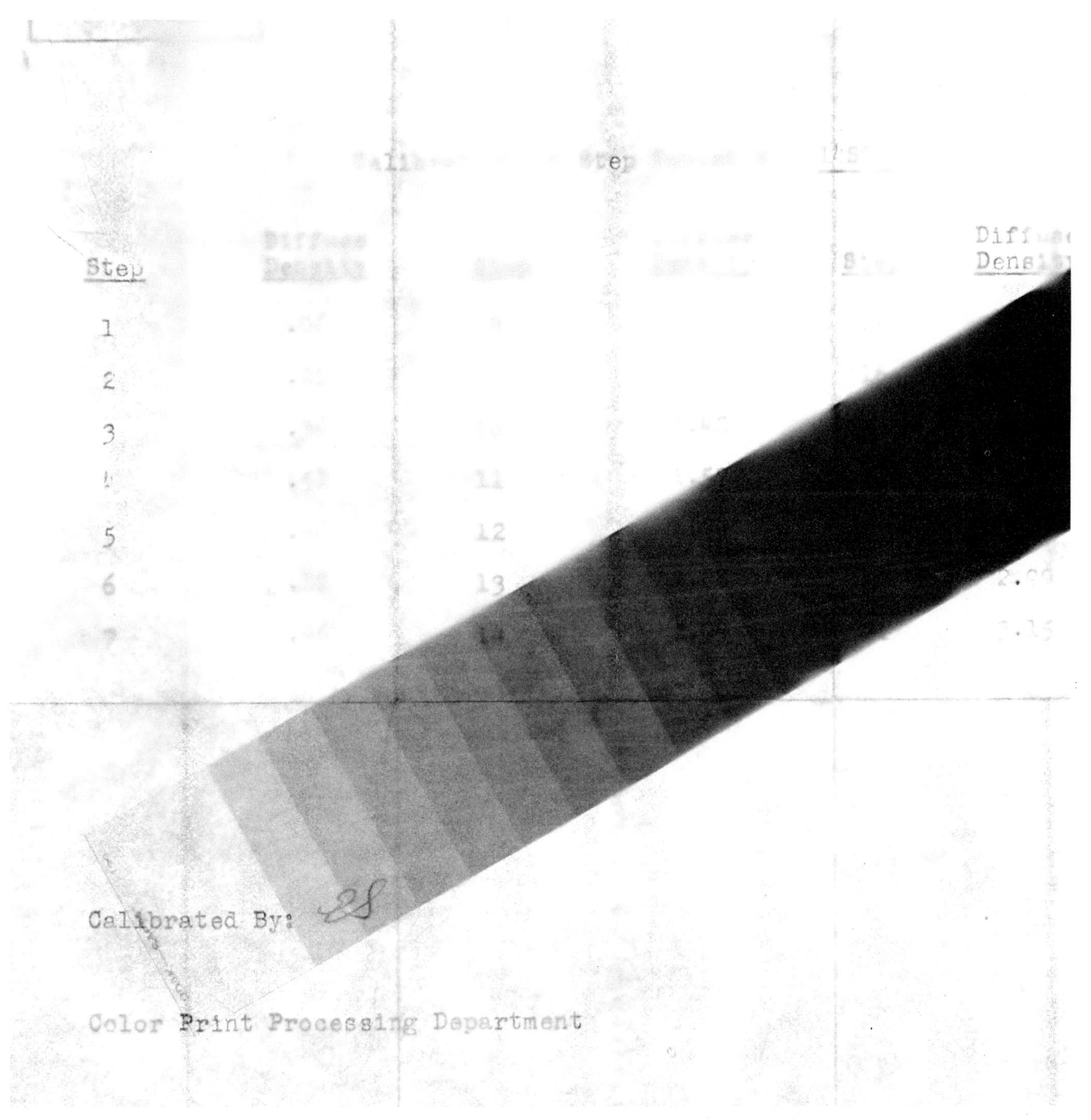

a calibrated density wedge illustrates the special tools needed to perfect advanced controls of photographic methods

3: advanced processes

INTRODUCTION TO THE ZONE SYSTEM

The Zone System is a method of calculating exposure and planning the development of negatives to produce a print with definite qualities. It embranes the negative, print, and photographic subject, linking them with common terms.

The Zone System dates from the early 1940's. Out of Ansel Adams' personal method of exposuring and developing he formulated the Zone System. The name arises from his simplification of the photographic grey scale. Adams provided names for areas of the scale. The greys are ten distinct tones between black and white. These steps replace the smooth grey scale and permit us to name a specific area. Being able to name it we can refer to it in the print, the negative, or the original subject.

To use the System, one must learn what the names mean. When a name is mentioned, a mental image of that specific grey must appear in the mind's eye.

The Zone System permits a photographer to calculate exposures while in front of the photographic subject knowing that after exposure and development he can produce a print with certain tones. The image becomes a predictable photographic equivalent of what the photographer sees when he looks at the subject. After preliminary testing of his materials and equipment the photographer is free of most risks of trial-and-error.

For other information on the Zone System read Minor White's *The Zone System Manual* (Morgan and Morgan). Also see Ansel Adams' *Basic Photo Series* (Morgan and Morgan).

One use for the system is to predict the effect of exposure and development on a film. Another is predicting certain tones in the print before the photograph is exposed. A third is learning to previsualize changes possible if one wishes to depart from naturalistic renderings.

The Zone System is a tool. It permits accurate control of film, exposure, metering, and development. It permits accurate previsualization. It has great power as a nominative tool. One can name the parts of a picture which are most difficult to deal with, the individual grey tones. By naming them one can control them. It permits evaluation of any step in the photographic process, from the print to the negative, and to the exposure that produced it.

Between black and white are an infinite number of individual grey tones. These may be simplified to ten shades. Each of these ten shades is a "Zone". A Zone requires exactly twice as much exposure as the next lower Zone, anywhere in the scale.

For example, a negative is exposed to produce an all-over Zone V grey tone and then printed normally so that tone is realized. A second negative is exposed for exactly one more *f*-stop. Printing the second negative exactly as the first results in a Zone VI area on the print. The two grey tones are one Zone apart visually and are produced by negatives that are one *f*-stop apart in exposure.

Because of the nature of exposure-density relationships of film and paper, the grey areas called Zones are not evenly spaced. They fall into three main groups.

LOW ZONES

ZONES 0, I, II, and III are: the maximum black of the paper, almost black, very dark, and dark. Contemporary enlarging papers cannot differentiate 0 and I in practice, although these densities can be established on the negatives.

MIDDLE ZONES

ZONES IV, V, and VI are: dark grey, middle grey, and light grey. Zone V is the color of the Kodak Greycard (18% reflectance); Zone VI is often compared to average skin tone (caucasian) or to north sky.

HIGH ZONES

ZONES VII, VIII, and IX are: light grey, pale grey, and white. Zone VII contains the last major surface details. Zone VIII contains the least perceptible detail.

Zone III is often referred to as the Darkest Detailed Shadow. At the other end of the scale Zone VII is called a Textured Highlight. Both of these names and the tones they represent are often misunderstood. Misunderstanding the name inhibits use of the System. Beginning photographers usually try to place fully textured light values in Zone VIII when they should be in Zone VII (e.g., light concrete).

The description of the tones is real. This is the way silver materials work, the way they look. The photographic grey scale crushes low tones and high tones. It is not neat equal steps, moving in a stately way from black to white. All the near-blacks fill up the bottom four Zones. The middle tones (where almost everything happens) is only three Zones. The light tones bunch together like the dark ones. It is not the distribution one might desire—it is what silver produces.

Most textures and important tones occur in the middle Zones. The dark and light Zones add brilliance and strength.

ZONES, FILM DENSITIES, AND GREY TONES

ZONE	DENSITIES 120	35-mm	DESCRIPTION	PHYSICALLY EQUIVALENT TONES
0	0.10	0.30	black	The blackest tone the paper will produce.
I	0.15	0.33	almost black	The least perceptible change from Zone 0.
II	0.30	0.37	very dark	On many papers this is the first change from 0.
III	0.45	0.45	grey-black	Areas of darkest detail in original subject.
IV	0.60	0.60	dark grey	Major important dark shadow areas.
V	0.75	0.75	MIDDLE GREY	Kodak Greycard (18% reflectance).
VI	0.95	0.90	light grey	Average skin tones (caucasian); photographic north sky.
VII	1.10	1.05	grey	Light textured concrete, highlighted skin.
VIII	1.30	1.20	off-white	Last sign of detail in the print.
IX	1.50	1.30	white	The clearest white the paper can make.
X	1.65	1.40	white+	The next Zone *in the negative*. Zone densities continue to build and can be printed by sacrificing the lower Zones, crushing them together in printing.

A WORKING METHOD WITH THE ZONE SYSTEM

The Zone System can be used to describe the tones of a print. It can describe the reflective values of the original subject, the mental image we hold of the subject, or the specific densities of the negative and the print. Its success requires careful metering of the light reflected from the photographic subject. The *Basic Photo Series* describe many of the special problems of correct metering.

The tones of the print are equivalent to the vocabulary and syntax of the poet; with these tones we communicate our thoughts through photography.

There are different methods of working out Zone controls for your equipment including: camera, meter, film, developer, agitation, enlarger, print paper, and developer. Other methods are outlined in the *Zone System Manual* and in the *Basic Photo Series*.

Step 1. Determine a System Index. This index of film sensitivity incorporates the camera, lens, meter and metering method with one development and agitation needed to produce a safe minimum-density negative.

1a. Use a Kodak Greycard (18% side) as a target. Photograph it in even light. There must be no direct reflections from the slightly glossy surface of the card toward the lens. Focus the camera on "infinity". The image of the greycard will be out of focus, reducing the chances of smudges affecting the image; and there will be no "bellows extension" exposure correction. Fill the viewfinder of the camera completely with the image of the greycard.

1b. Meter the greycard. Calculate an exposure based on this reading, and then actually expose four *f*-numbers less than the indicated exposure. Using the exposure indicated by the meter would merely place the card in Zone V. Closing down the iris four *f*-numbers will place the exposure in Zone I, i.e. one stop above the film-base-plus-fog density which is Zone 0.

1c. Make five exposures of the greycard. Alternate an exposure with an unexposed frame. (If a viewcamera is being used, simply pull the darkslide halfway out.)

The first exposure will be made at 3 times the Manufacturer's Index.

The second exposure at 1½ times the suggested Index.

The third exposure at the suggested Index.

The fourth exposure at ¾ the suggested Index.

The last exposure at ½ the suggested Index.

1d. Develop the film according to a Standard Development Method.

1e. When the film is dry, examine it. There will be a frame that is light grey but definitely denser than the unexposed frames. There will be other frames that are much darker than the blank frames. One or more frames may disappear. These were exposed at too high an index and were below the threshold of sensitivity of that film. The frame that is fully perceptible is the indicator of the System Index. This is the meter index to use with your equipment to produce a negative with the least density yet which produces safe printing values for a carefully metered scene.

A frame may appear clearly defined to your eye, yet not print at all. This is an unusable indication of the Index threshold.

Step 2. Determine a Standard Enlarger Time

2a. Raise the enlarger lamphouse to produce an 8×10 patch of light on the easel. In all the *Handbook* tests it is assumed that a correct lens and film carriage are in the enlarger and that the image of the edge of the film carriage is focused. This will produce brightnesses equivalent to actual working conditions.

2b. Set the lens at *f*-11. Expose a piece of 4×5 inch paper under the enlarger for 30 seconds. Develop this for 3 minutes in the recommended developer dilution. This piece of paper is now a **Standard Black Patch.**

2c. Put the film produced above in the film carriage. Project it so the minimum density frame and part of the adjacent blank frame show.

2d. Expose sheets of normal contrast grade paper. Begin with 3 second exposures, and double each sequential exposure. Mark each sheet carefully with a pencil. Finally, develop them all together. Develop four sheets for three minutes at 70 degrees.

2e. Dry the test sheets and examine them to discover which has a real, but minimum perceptible change of density between the image of the blank frame and the image of the minimum density frame. The test may have to be repeated at smaller intervals to discover the exact time needed. This is the **Standard Enlarger Time.**

Step. 3. Determine a Normal Development Time for Film. Normal development by the comparison method will produce a negative that prints on normal contrast grade paper to yield a Zone V print value when the Zone I exposure is correctly placed (according to the System Index established in the first step). This is the keystone of the Zone System. It is based on the fact that the longer a negative is developed the more dense will become the highlight values in the negative. If increased development made all exposed areas more dense proportionately, then the Zone System controls would not exist. Increased development causes increased density range.

3a. Meter a greycard (as in Step 1). Place the exposure normally to produce a Zone V grey value density in the negative.

3b. Expose three rolls of film identically. Alternate exposures with unexposed frames.

3c. Develop the first roll at the time suggested in the Standard Development Method. Complete the processing of the film.

3d. Print one of the negatives from the first third at Standard Enlarger Time. Process and dry the print. Compare the grey tone produced on the print with the greycard used as a target. They may be viewed through a yellow filter to eliminate the differences in blue-grey coloration. If they compare closely, the development time is NORMAL. If the image is too light, the development time must be decreased. If the image is dark, the time must be increased.

3e. If the image was too light, decrease the development time 10% and develop a second film. Verify the new development time to be Normal. The third film is for insurance, if anything is wrong with the processing of the first.

Step 4. Determining an Expansion Development. As development increases there is a corresponding increase of highlight densities but no marked increase in shadow density.

4a. Find and photograph what is called a "nine Zone" subject. A Normal subject has a metering range ten *f*-numbers long. If the important highlight area (VIII) is metered, and the darkest detailed shadow (III) is metered, then there should be five *f*-numbers between them for a scene requiring a Normal development. If, however, a scene is metered and the important highlight area is only four *f*-numbers different from the darkest detailed shadow area exposure, the total range of the scene is nine Zones, rather than ten. Expose for the shadowed area; increase development. This will permit the negative to be printed on Normal contrast paper.

Find a flat-lighted subject. Meter the "darkest detailed shadow" and write down the exposure indicated. Call that area Zone III. Meter the "highest textured highlight" and write down that exposure. When choosing possible exposure combinations select those which have the same exposure time.

> For example, the dark exposure is ¼ second at *f*-4, and the high value exposure ¼ second at *f*-22. Count the number of *f*-stops between the indicated exposures. Each *f*-stop interval corresponds to a Zone:

f-3	*f*-5.6	*f*-8	*f*-11	*f*-16	*f*-22	*f*-32	
III	IV	V	VI	VII	VIII	IX	etc.

The metered intervals in this example describe a "normal" scene of ten Zones, i.e., one which has five *f*-number intervals between what should be Zone III and what should be Zone VIII. If, however, the highest textured highlight exposure had not metered *f*-22 but only *f*-16, the scene would need extra development. Increasing development is called *expanding* the density range or *expansion development.*

4b. Meter the darkest shadow areas which must have detail. Expose two *f*-stops less than the indicated exposure. Develop the film longer than normal time. High speed films (Index = 400) will need about 30% more development. Medium speed films (Index = 125) will require about 20% more development than normal. Low speed films (Index = 32) will require only 10% more development. These are trial development times. Print the negatives to verify that these do in fact produce full-scale, full-substance images on normal grade paper, printed at or near Standard Enlarger Time.

Step. 5. Determining other Development Times, for other Expansions and Contractions. For a given scene there will be an appropriate development plan. Find a seven zone scene; expand the development time for a percentage similar to that used for the first test. Verify by printing. Do the same for contractions. Find a long-scale scene, where the metered exposure indications are six *f*-numbers apart. Such a scene will require a shortened development time. Highspeed films will require less change of development than low speed films. The exposure is always controlled by metering shadow areas. Development is always controlled by the range between the shadow and the highlight exposures.

DENSITOMETRY AND PARAMETRIC CURVES

The densitometer dismays most photographers. It is only an exposure meter and is a basic tool. There are two kinds of densitometers available. One uses a photosensitive cell to meter the light absorbed by the negative. The absorption is a real number called "density". The other kind of densitometer uses the human eye to compare two light sources. One of these is located under the film, the other behind a movable plastic filter of varying density. The filter is moved until the eye indicates the two lights are equal. The density is read from the position of the filter.

Electrical densitometers are made by many companies. Comparison densitometers are made both for enlarging exposure indications and for negative density measuring. The first kind is made by HEATH and by ANALITE. The second kind by KODAK. The Kodak Model 1 Densitometer uses the eye to compare two lights.

Densities of contemporary negatives range from about 0.10 to 3.00. The clear edge of the film from a viewcamera negative will have a density of 0.10. The clear film from the edge of a Tri-X 35-mm camera negative will have a density of 0.30. They differ because the films are made differently. In this case the Tri-X has a grey dye incorporated into the film.

The density of textured highlight areas will also differ from large negatives to small ones. Large negatives will have Zone VIII densities of about 1.30. The same image areas in a 35-mm negative will have a density of about 1.15. The less dense the negative, the finer the grain; the finer the grain, the greater the enlargement possible without granularity.

Using a densitometer is not essential for the beginning photographer. In advanced work it is desirable and will save time and prevent waste of material. Using a densitometer allows four rolls of film to be used in doing all the work accomplished by trial-and-error in the Zone System Calibration outlined earlier.

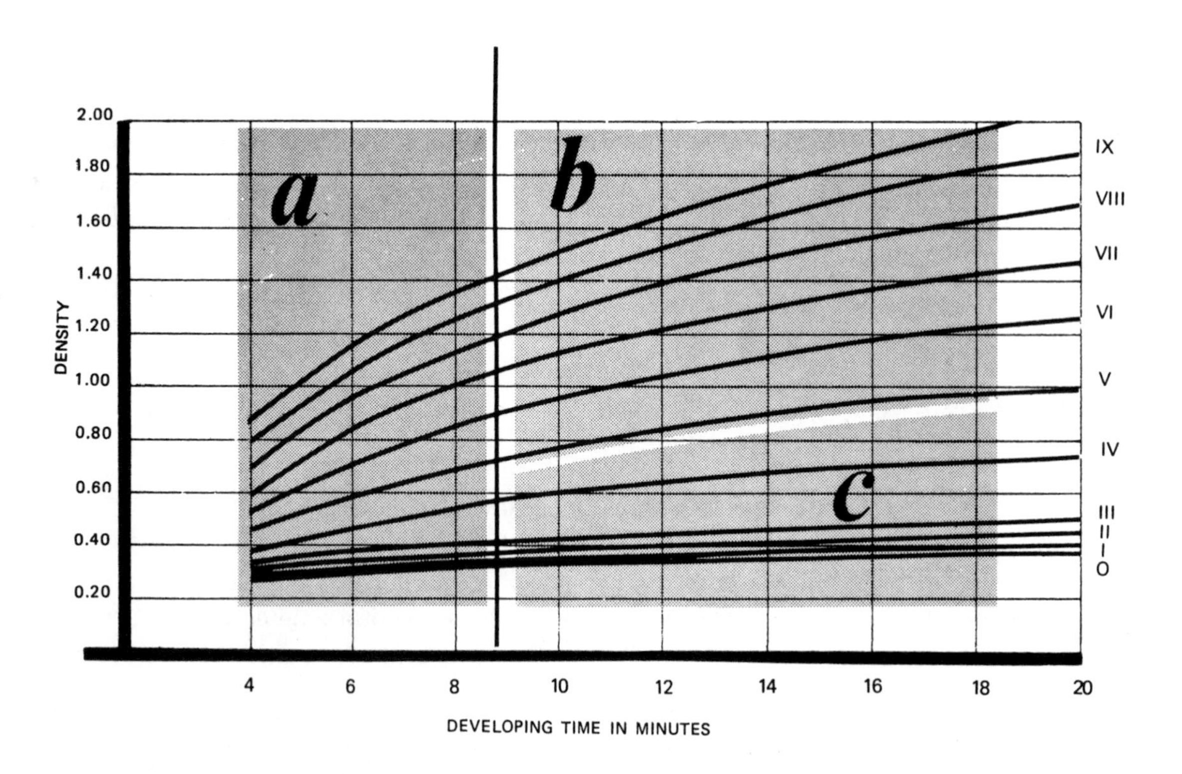

FIGURE 3-1. parametric curve analysis

a

b

c

SAMPLE EXPOSURE TABLE

SHEET	Exposure	Zone
1- a	1/50 f45	I
b	1/50 f45	II
c	1/50 f32	III
2-a	1/50 f16	IV
b	1/50 f16	V
c	1/50 f11	VI
3- a	1/50 f5.6	VII
b	1/50 f5.6	VIII
c	1/25 f5.6	IX
4- a	1/8 f5.6	X
b	1/8 f5.6	XI
c	1/4 f5.6	XII
edges	none	O

FIGURE 3-2. exposing large format films

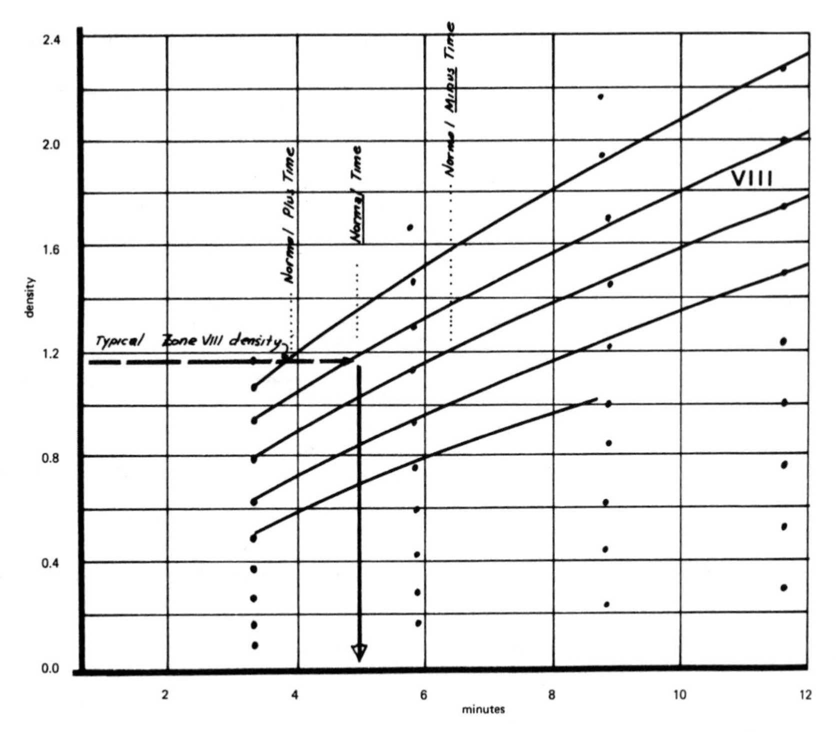

FIGURE 3-3. sample parametric curve construction

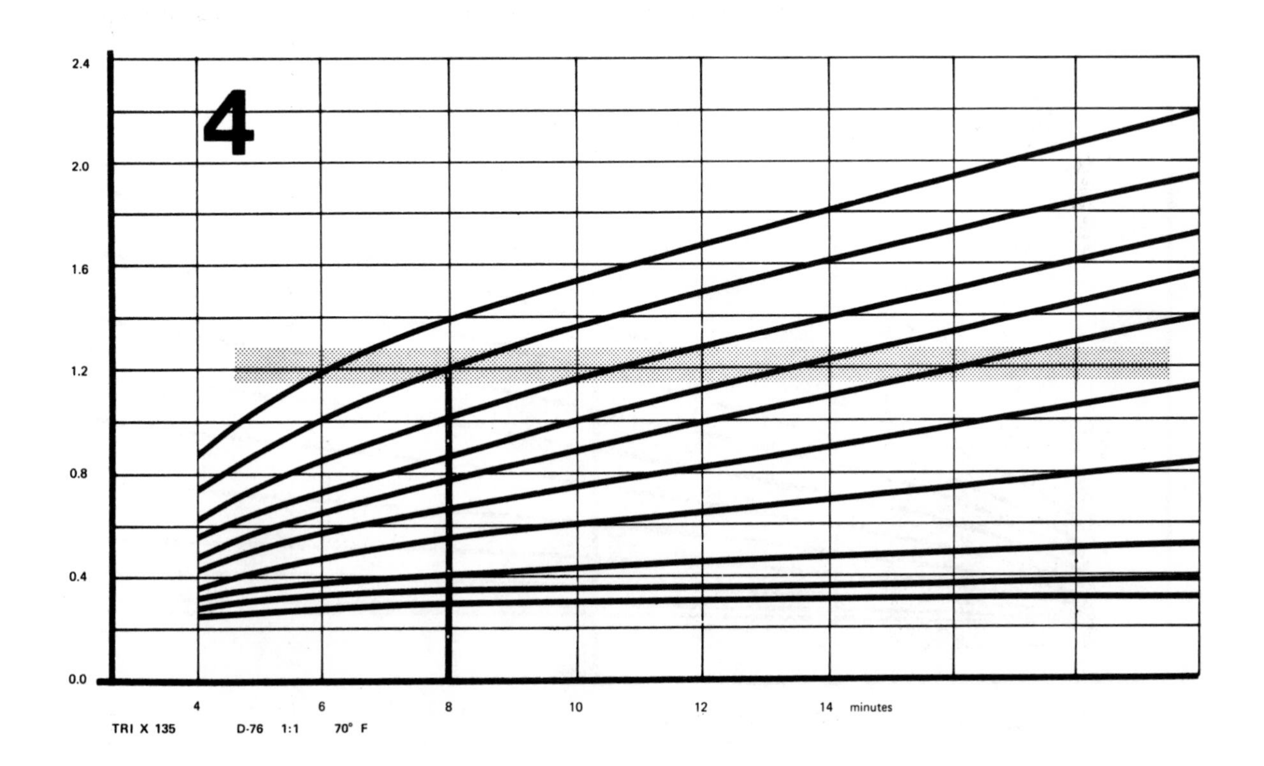

5

2.4
2.0
1.6
1.2
0.8
0.4
0.0

4 6 8 10 12 14 minutes

TRI X 135 HC 110 1:31 70° F

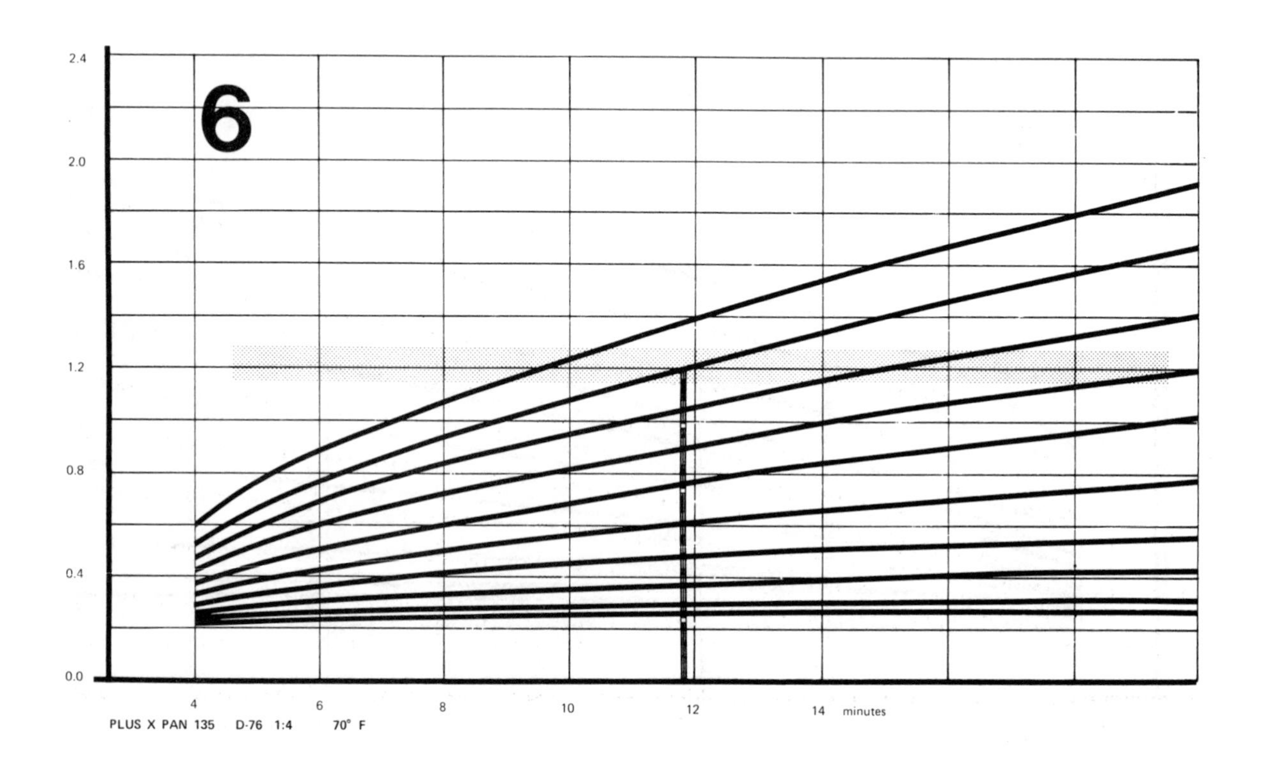

PLUS X PAN 135 D-76 1:4 70° F

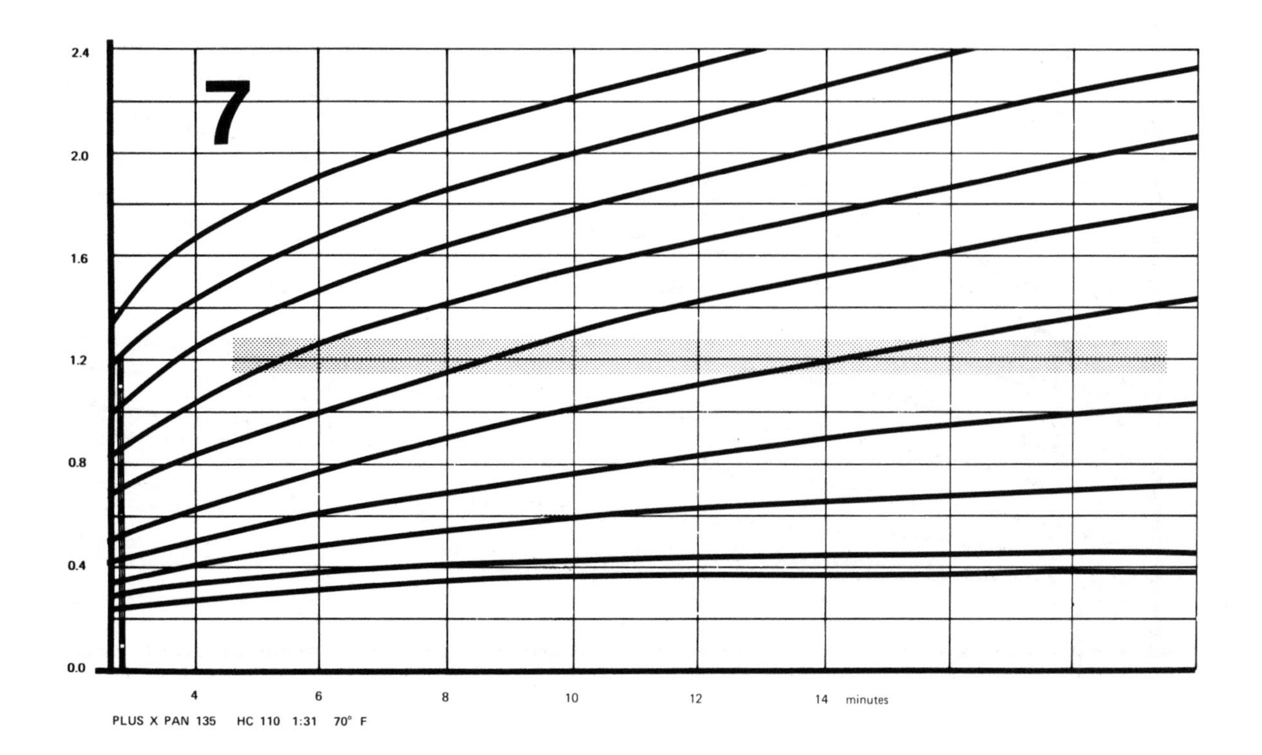
7
2.4
2.0
1.6
1.2
0.8
0.4
0.0
4
6
8
10
12
14 minutes
PLUS X PAN 135 HC 110 1:31 70° F

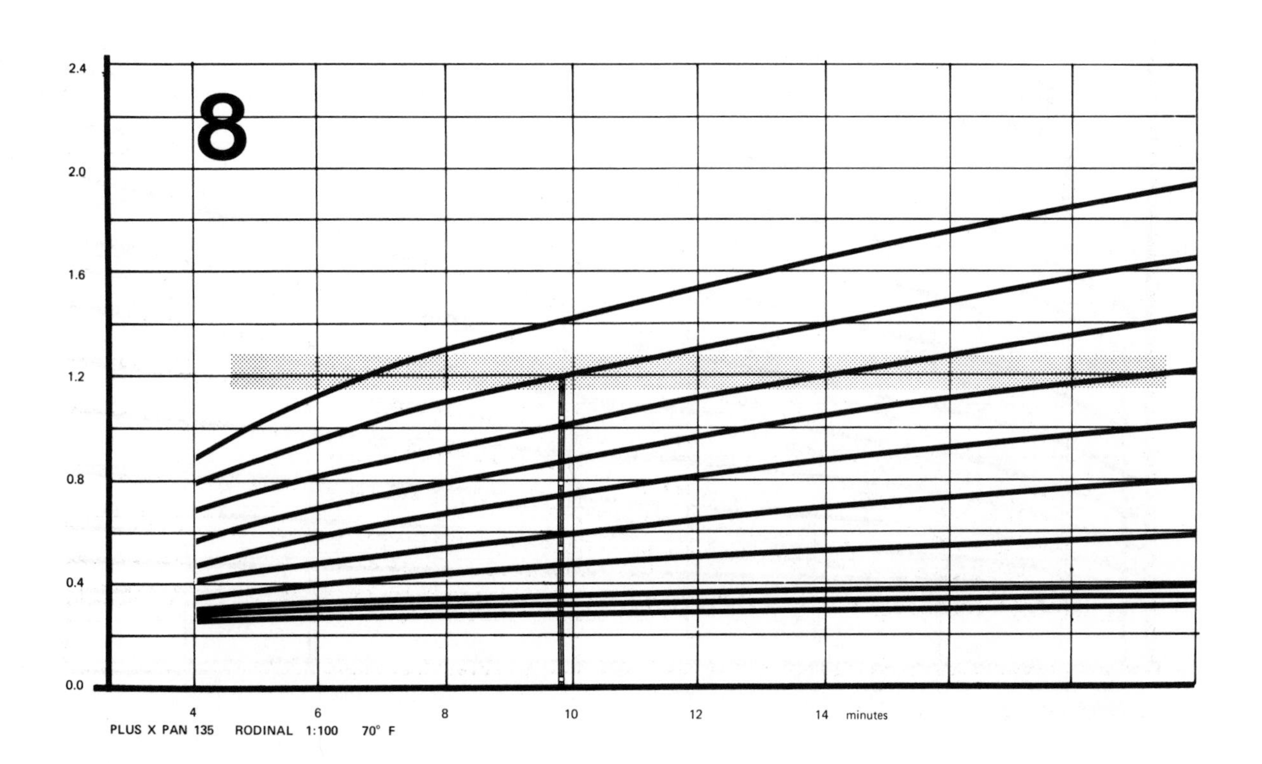
8
2.4
2.0
1.6
1.2
0.8
0.4
0.0
4
6
8
10
12
14 minutes
PLUS X PAN 135 RODINAL 1:100 70° F

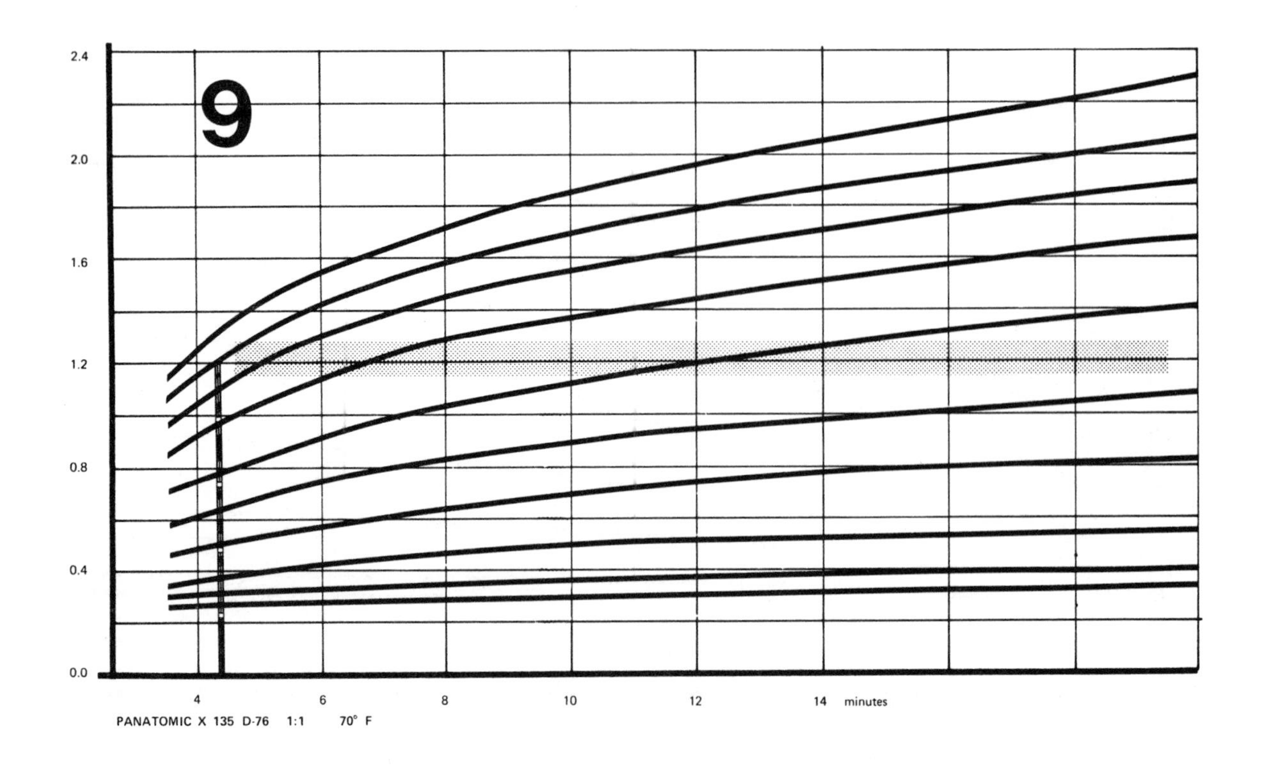
9
2.4
2.0
1.6
1.2
0.8
0.4
0.0
4
6
8
10
12
14 minutes
PANATOMIC X 135 D-76 1:1 70° F

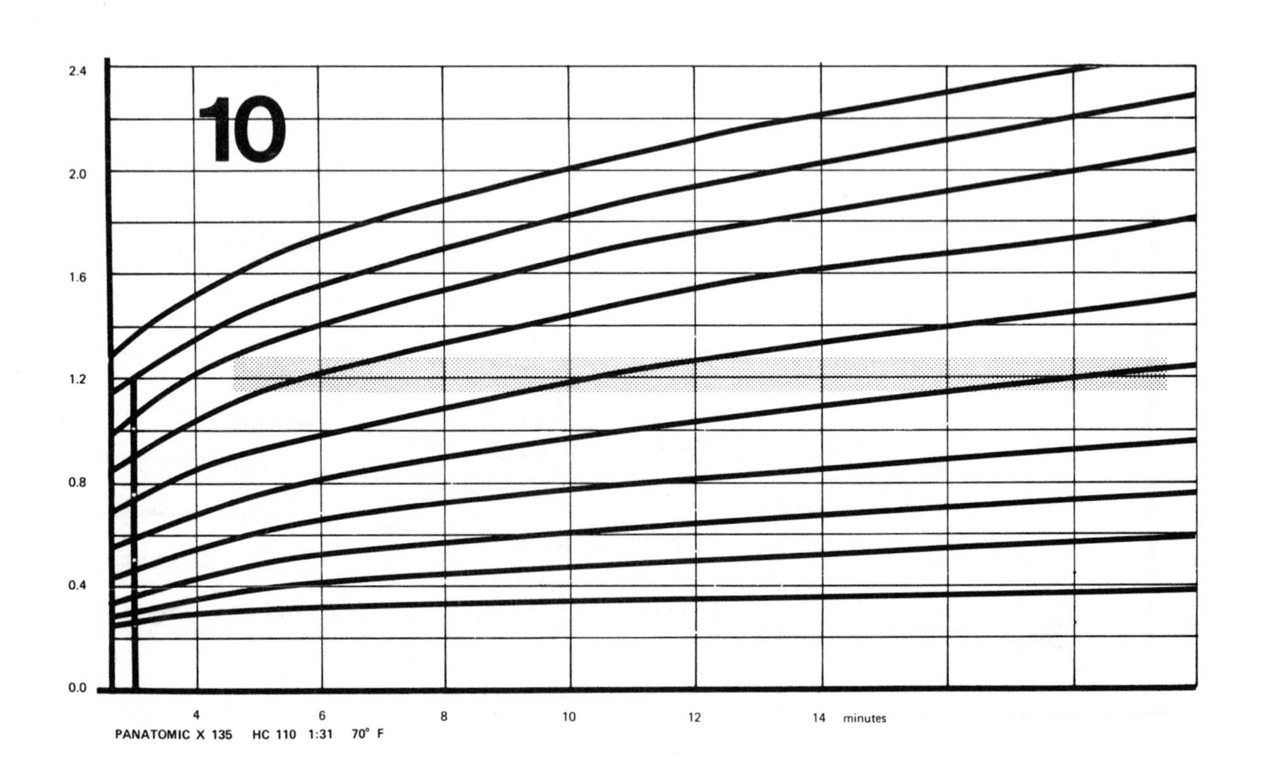
10
2.4
2.0
1.6
1.2
0.8
0.4
0.0
4
6
8
10
12
14 minutes
PANATOMIC X 135 HC 110 1:31 70° F

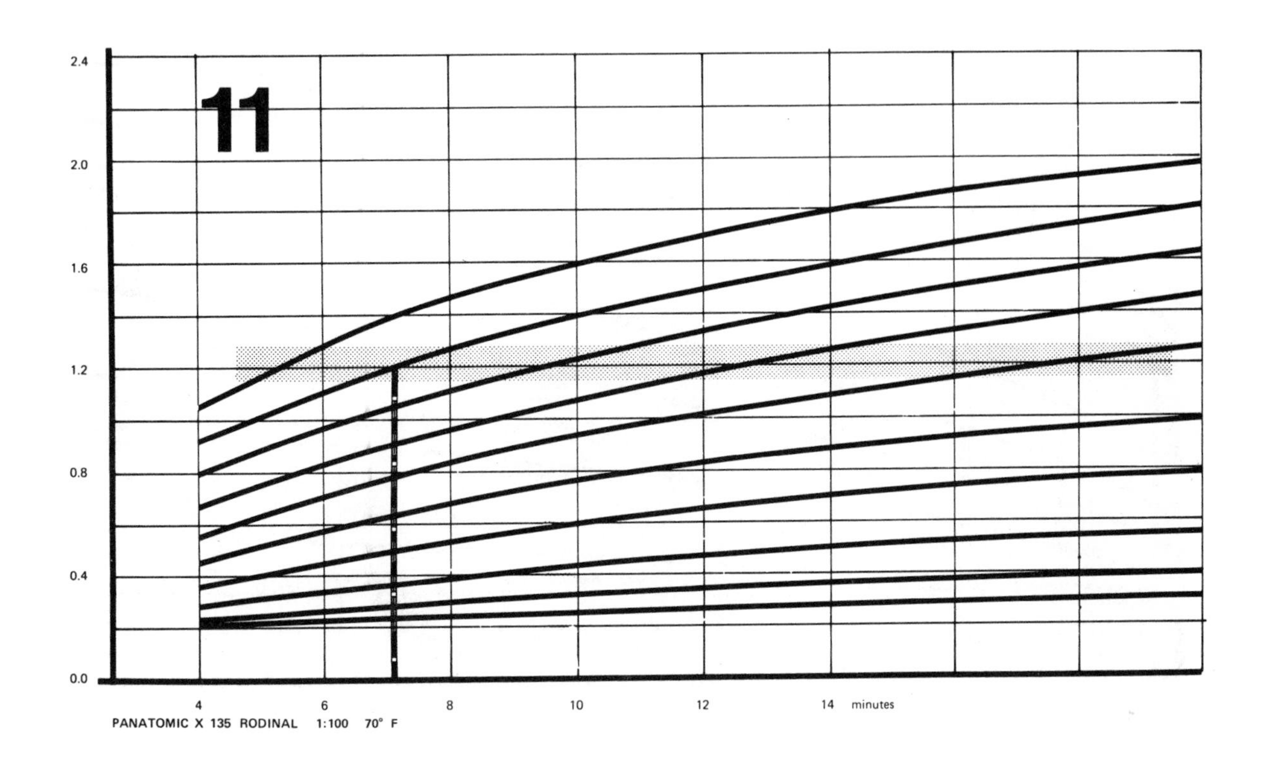
11
2.4
2.0
1.6
1.2
0.8
0.4
0.0
4
6
8
10
12
14 minutes
PANATOMIC X 135 RODINAL 1:100 70° F

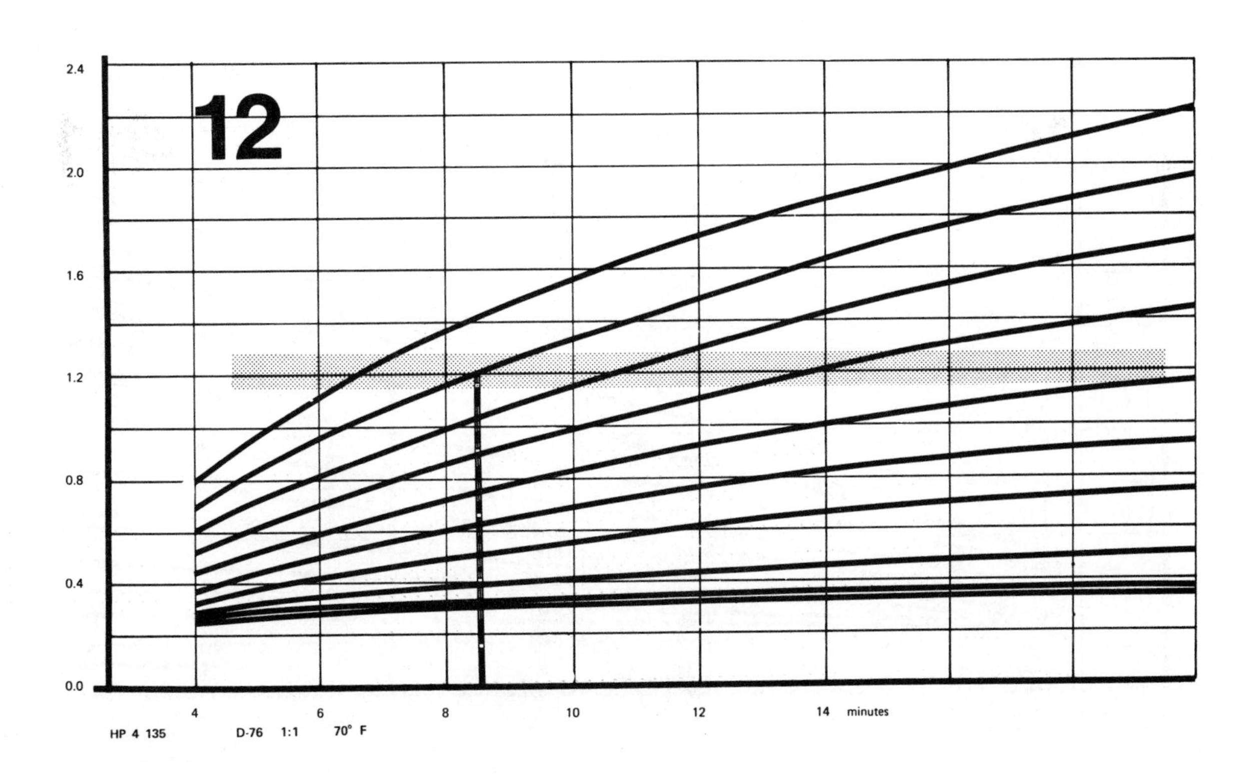
12
2.4
2.0
1.6
1.2
0.8
0.4
0.0
4
6
8
10
12
14 minutes
HP 4 135 D-76 1:1 70° F

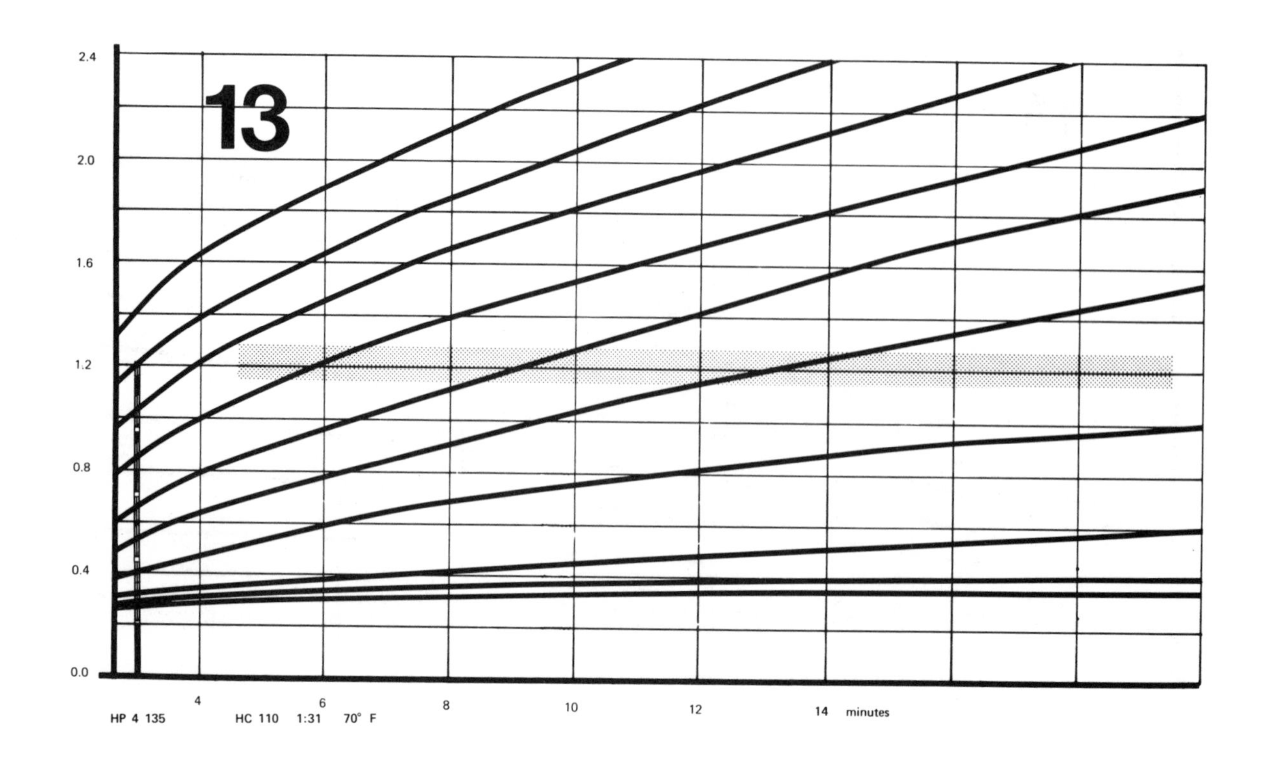
13
2.4
2.0
1.6
1.2
0.8
0.4
0.0
4
6
8
10
12
14 minutes
HP 4 135
HC 110 1:31 70° F

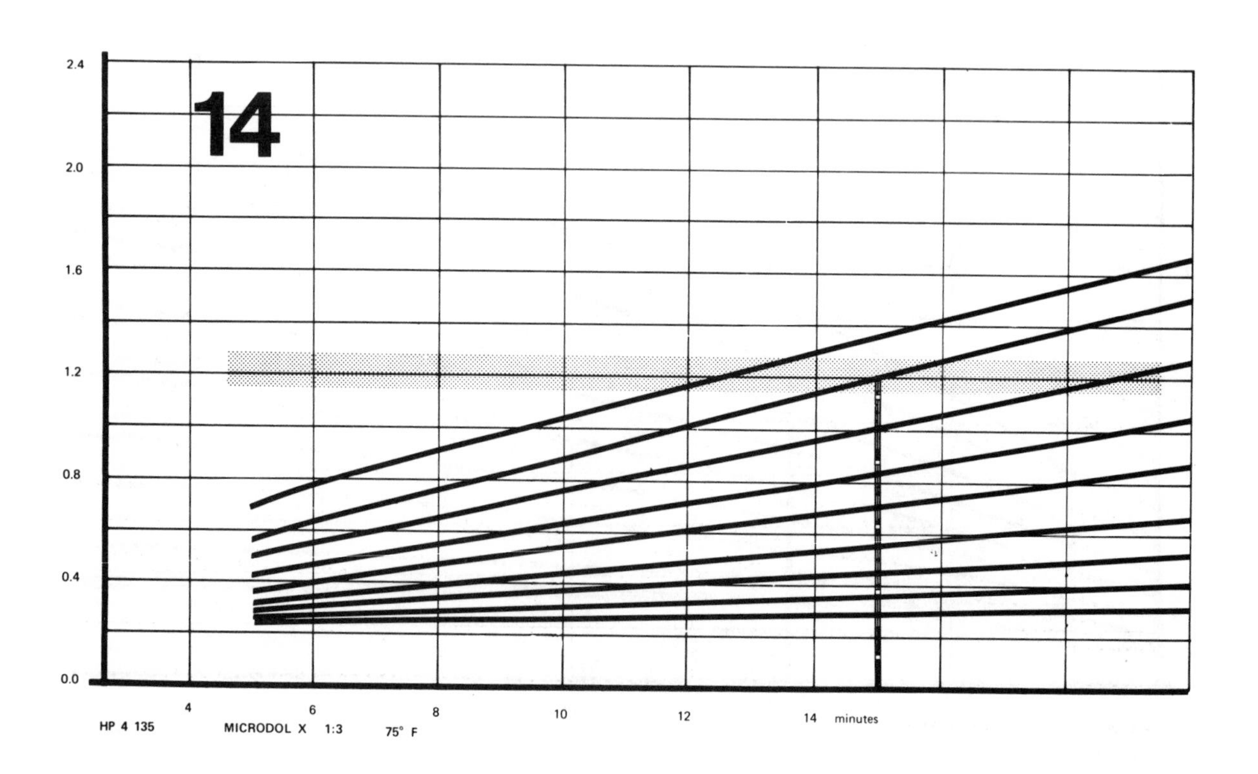
14
2.4
2.0
1.6
1.2
0.8
0.4
0.0
4
6
8
10
12
14 minutes
HP 4 135
MICRODOL X 1:3 75° F

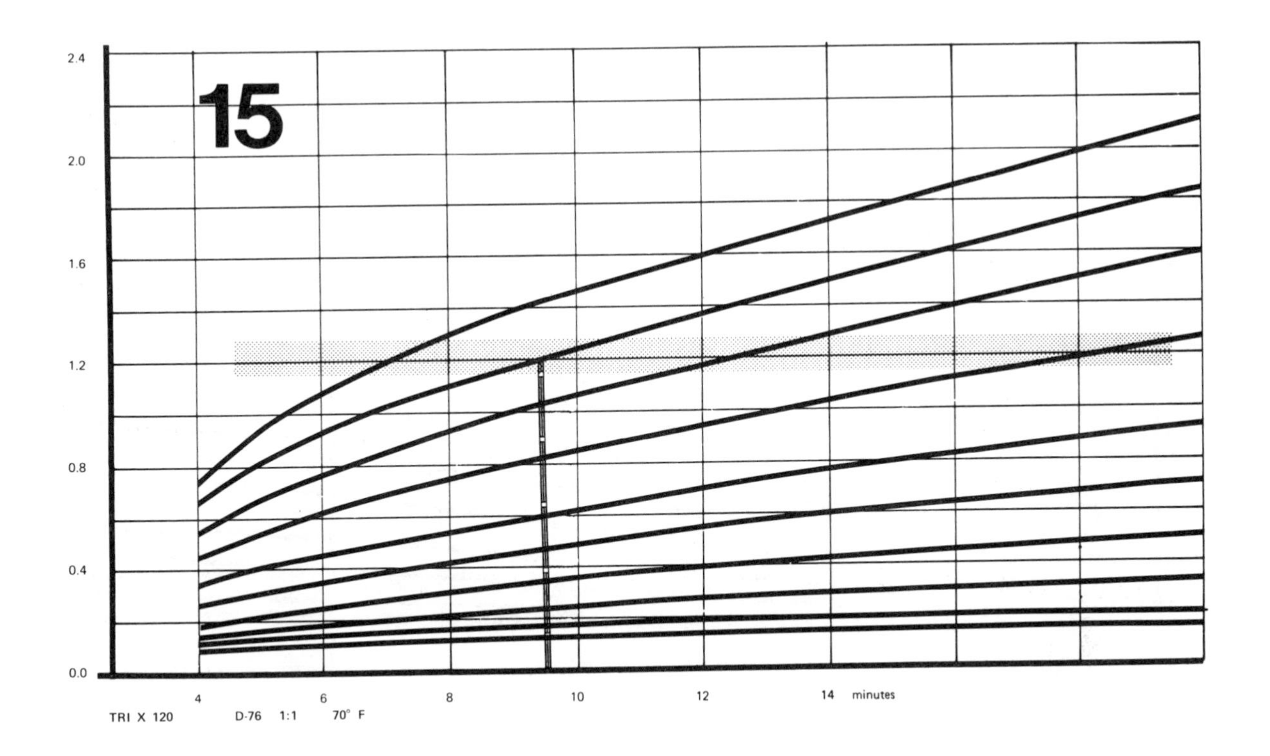
15
2.4
2.0
1.6
1.2
0.8
0.4
0.0
4
6
8
10
12
14 minutes
TRI X 120
D-76 1:1 70° F

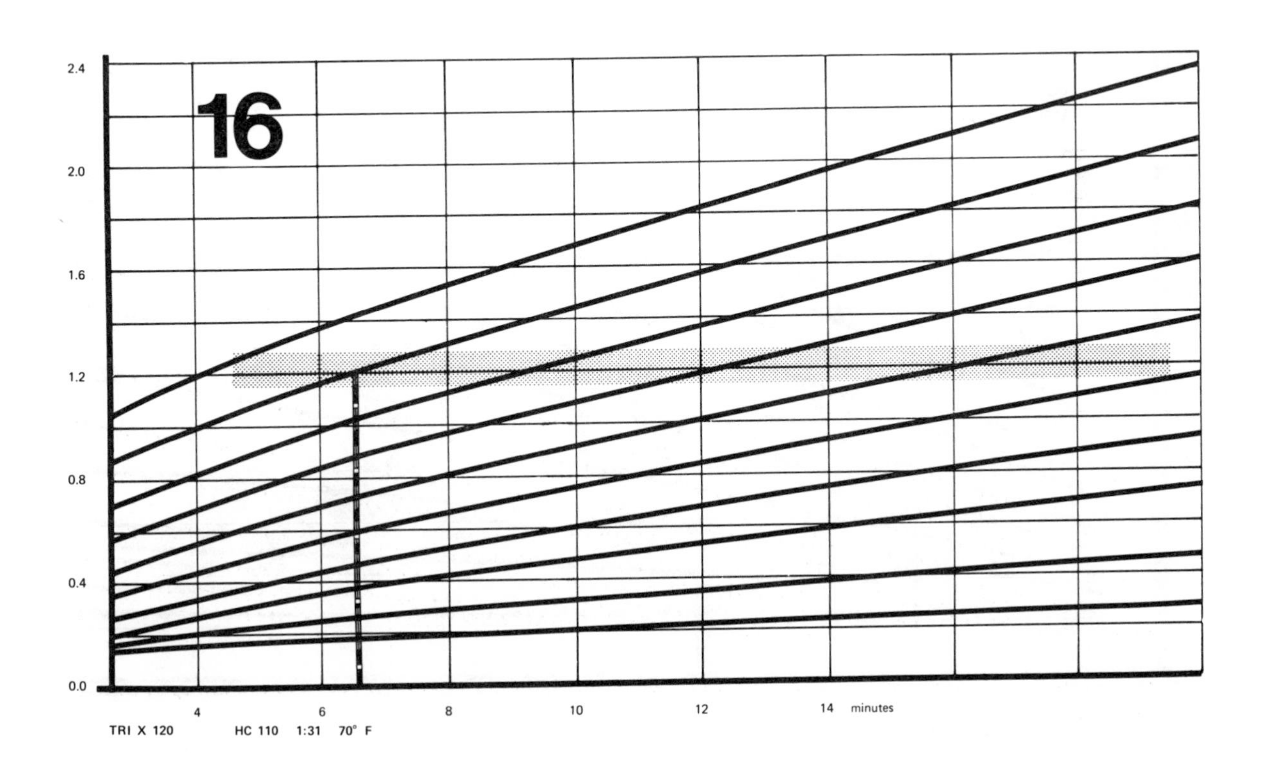
16
2.4
2.0
1.6
1.2
0.8
0.4
0.0
4
6
8
10
12
14 minutes
TRI X 120
HC 110 1:31 70° F

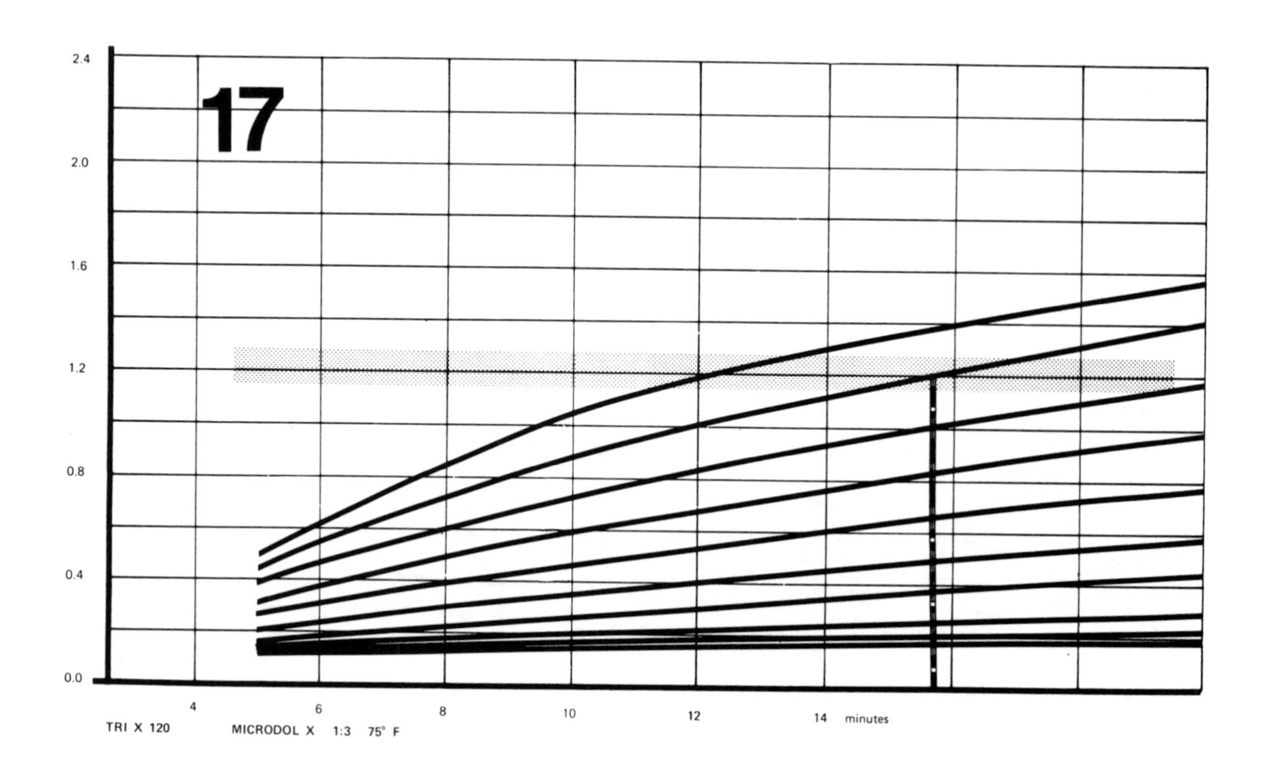
17
2.4
2.0
1.6
1.2
0.8
0.4
0.0
4
6
8
10
12
14 minutes
TRI X 120
MICRODOL X 1:3 75° F

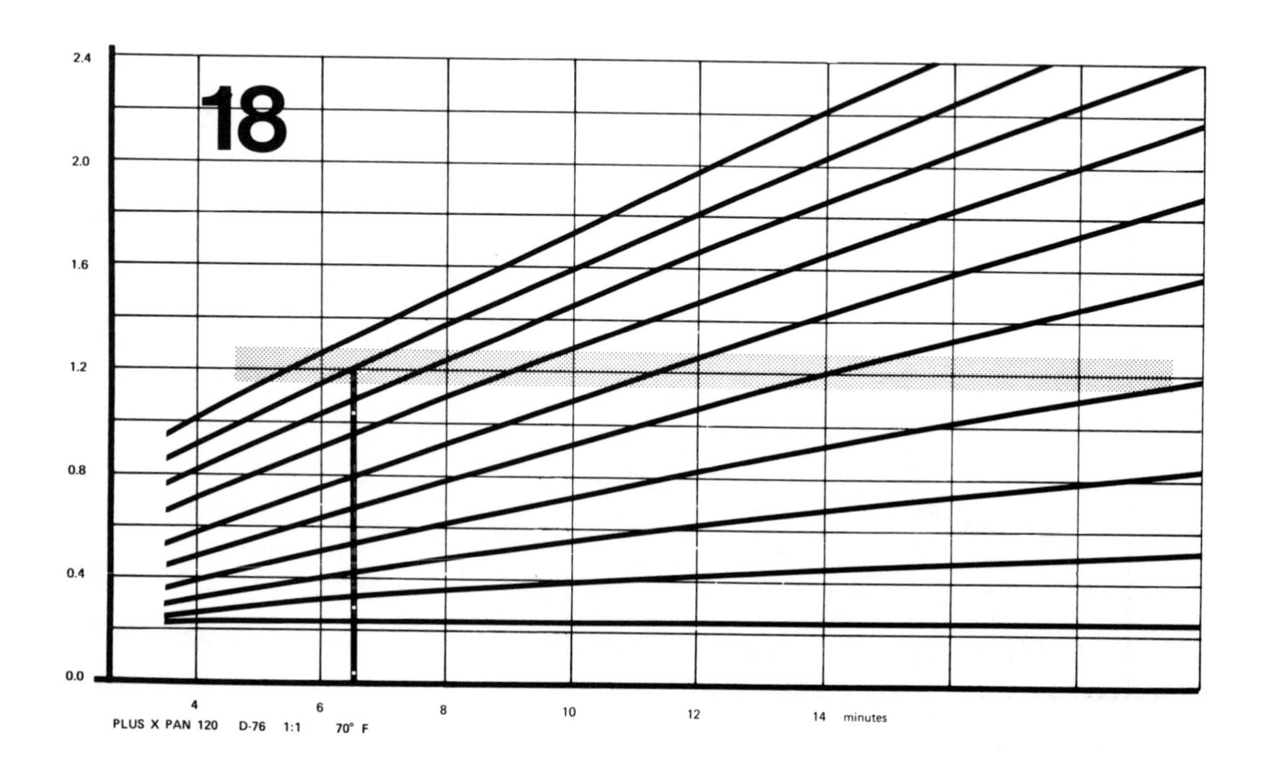
18
2.4
2.0
1.6
1.2
0.8
0.4
0.0
4
6
8
10
12
14 minutes
PLUS X PAN 120 D-76 1:1 70° F

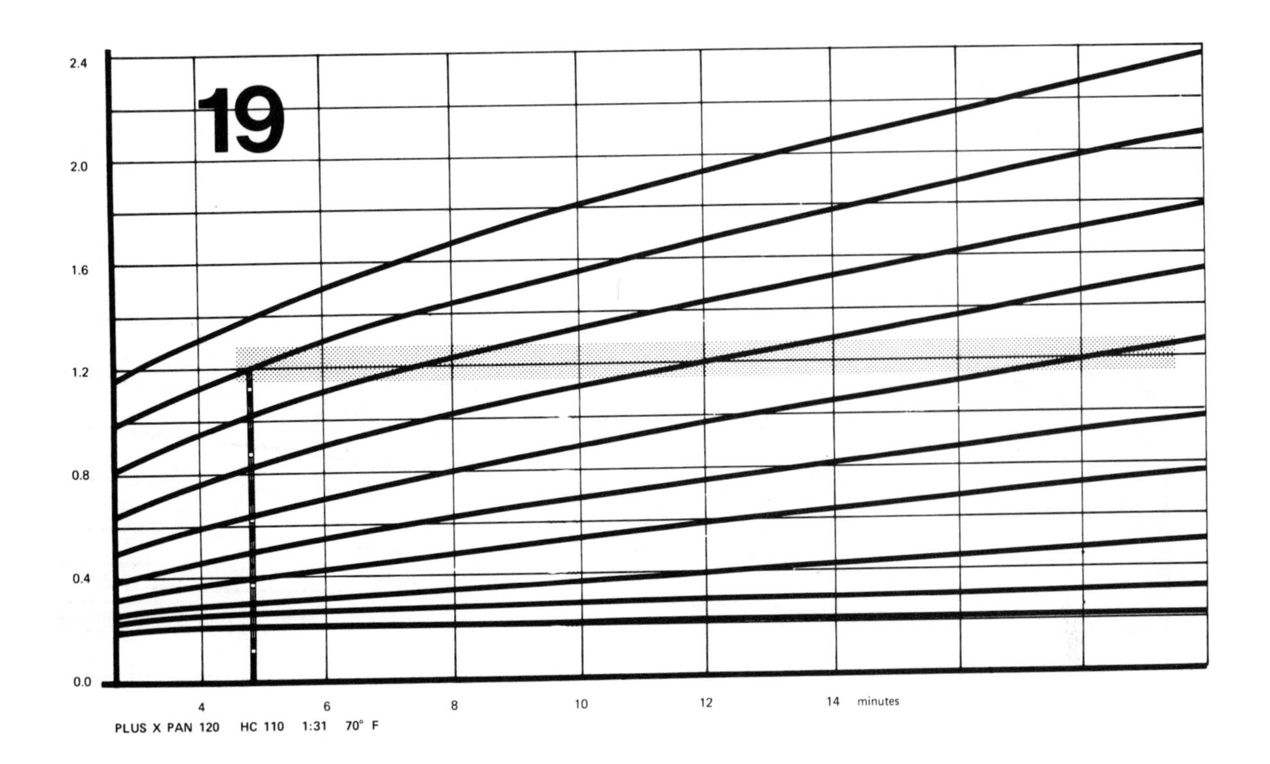
19
2.4
2.0
1.6
1.2
0.8
0.4
0.0
4
6
8
10
12
14 minutes
PLUS X PAN 120 HC 110 1:31 70° F

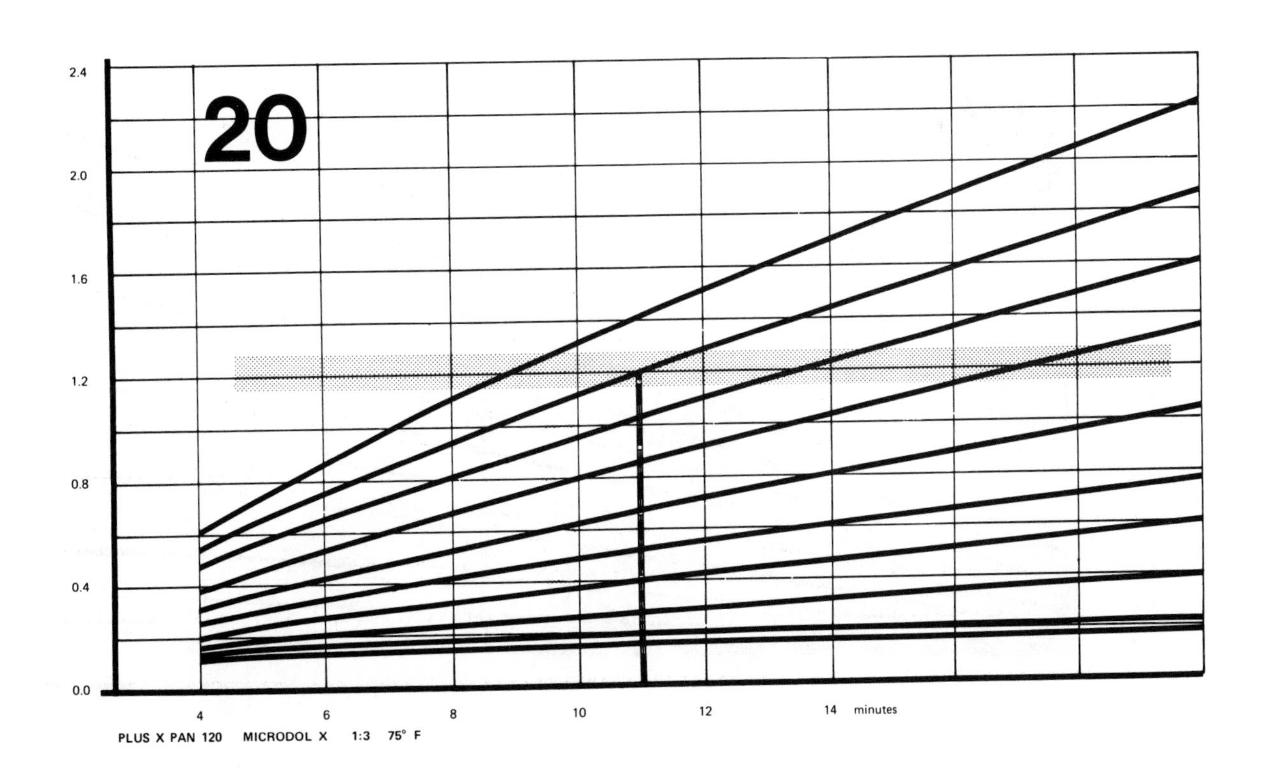
20
2.4
2.0
1.6
1.2
0.8
0.4
0.0
4
6
8
10
12
14 minutes
PLUS X PAN 120 MICRODOL X 1:3 75° F

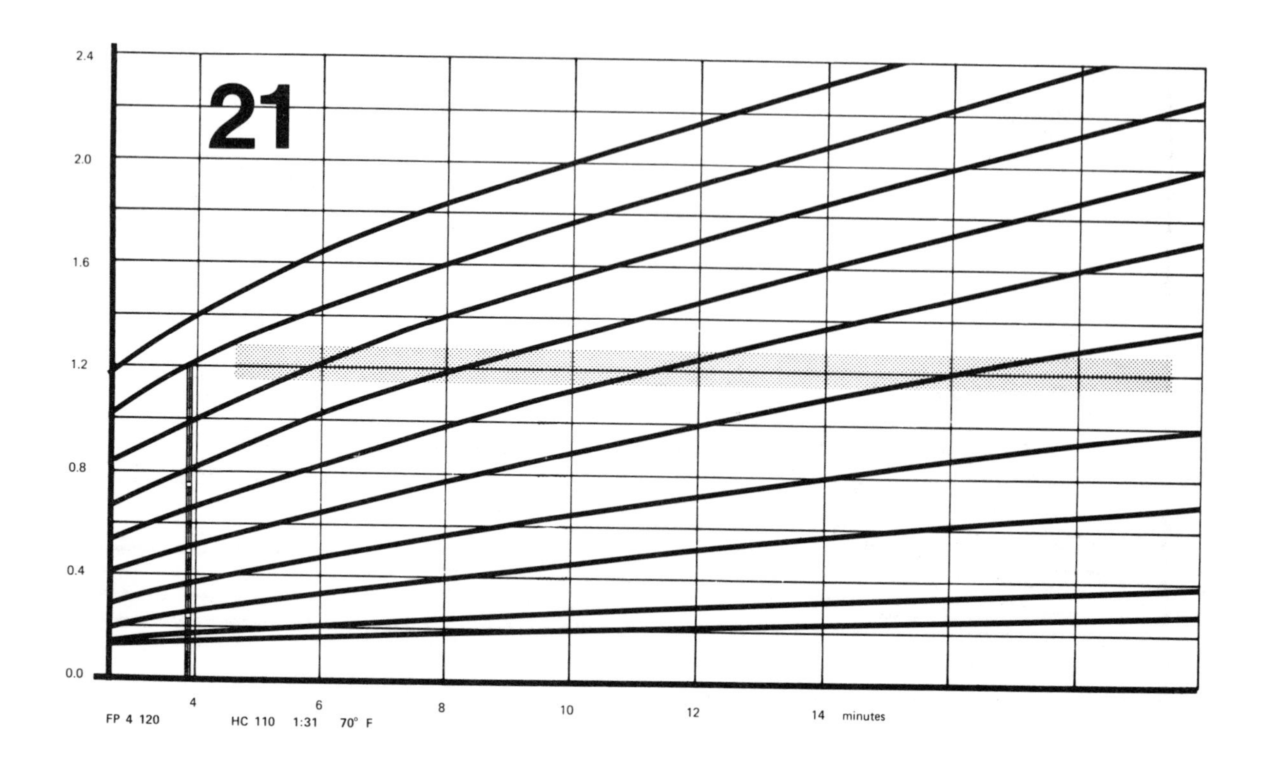
21
2.4
2.0
1.6
1.2
0.8
0.4
0.0
4
6
8
10
12
14 minutes
FP 4 120
HC 110 1:31 70° F

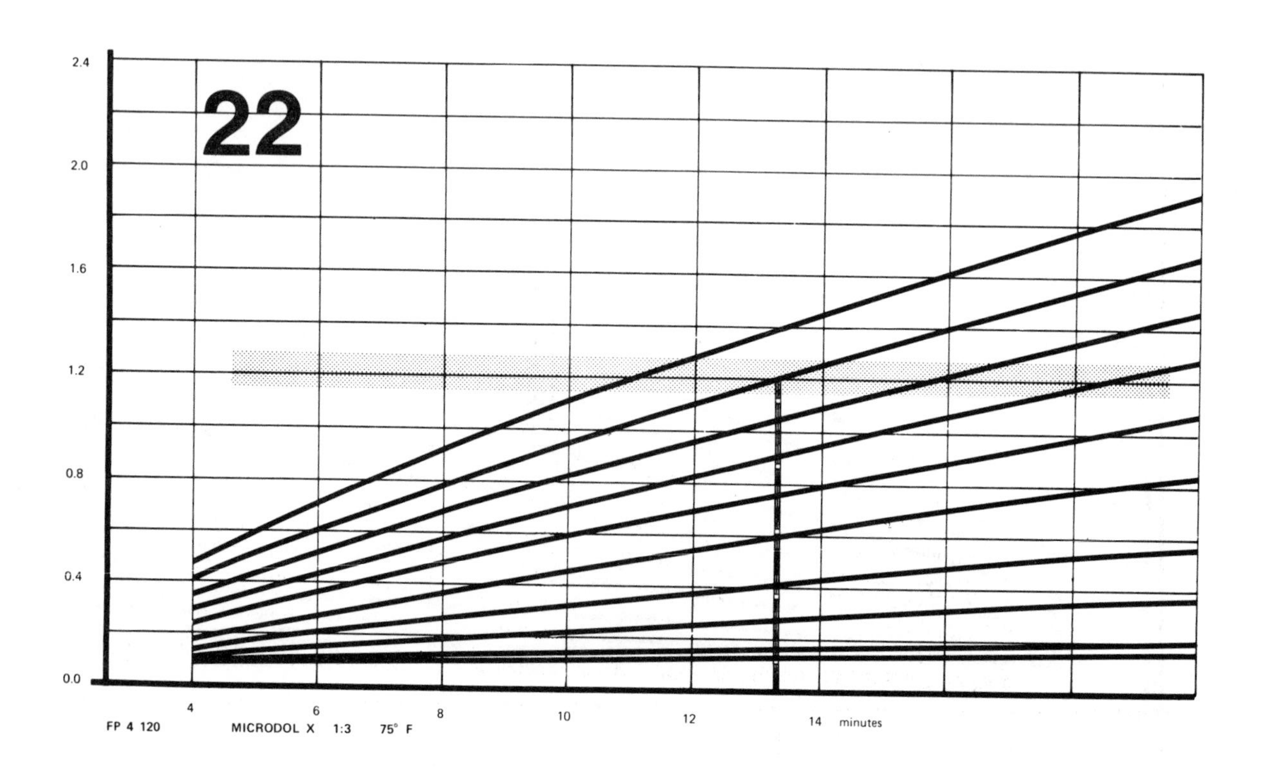
22
2.4
2.0
1.6
1.2
0.8
0.4
0.0
4
6
8
10
12
14 minutes
FP 4 120
MICRODOL X 1:3 75° F

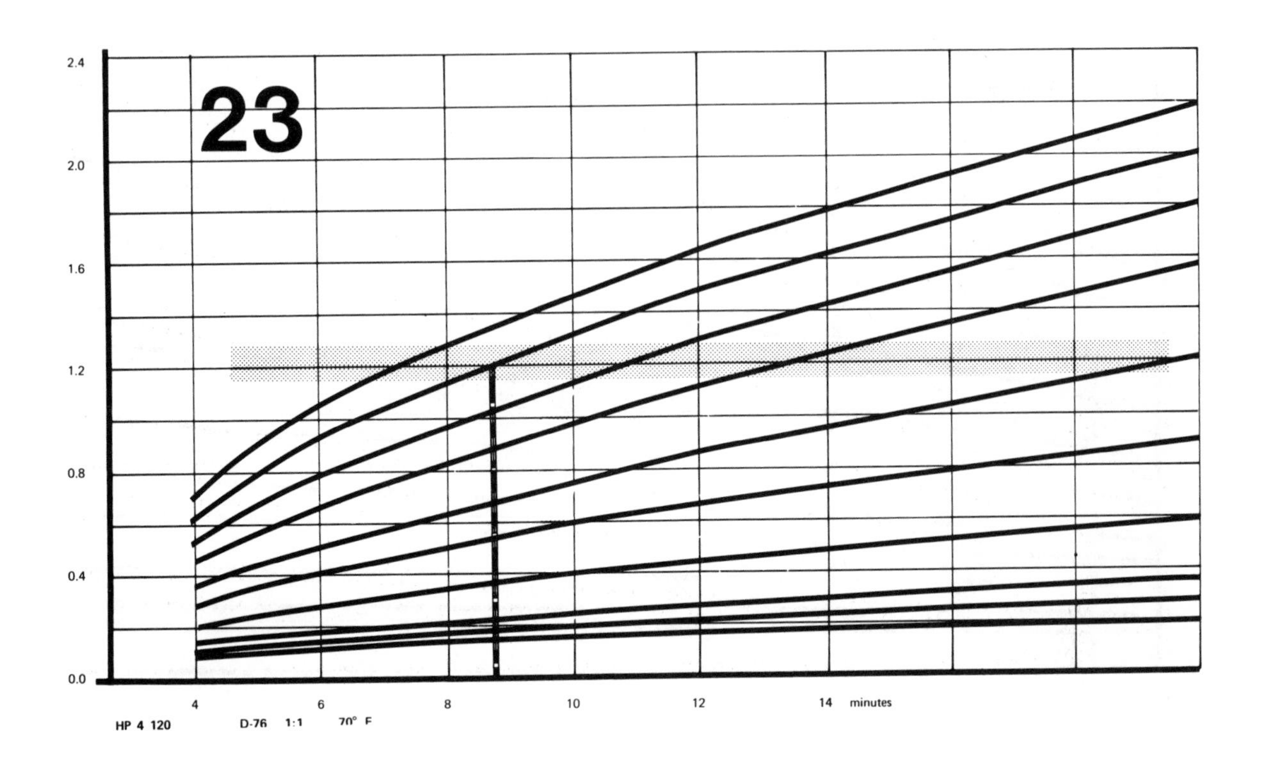
23
2.4
2.0
1.6
1.2
0.8
0.4
0.0
4
6
8
10
12
14 minutes
HP 4 120
D-76 1:1 70° F

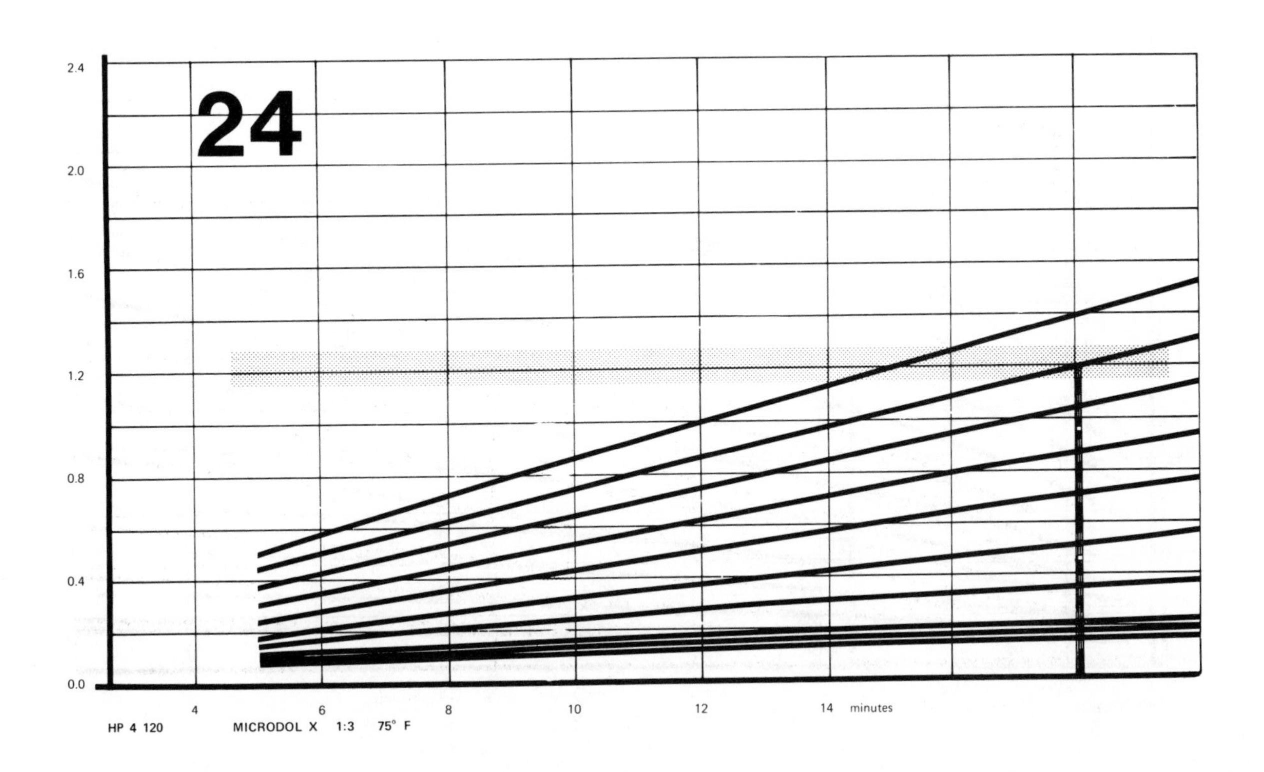
24
2.4
2.0
1.6
1.2
0.8
0.4
0.0
4
6
8
10
12
14 minutes
HP 4 120
MICRODOL X 1:3 75° F

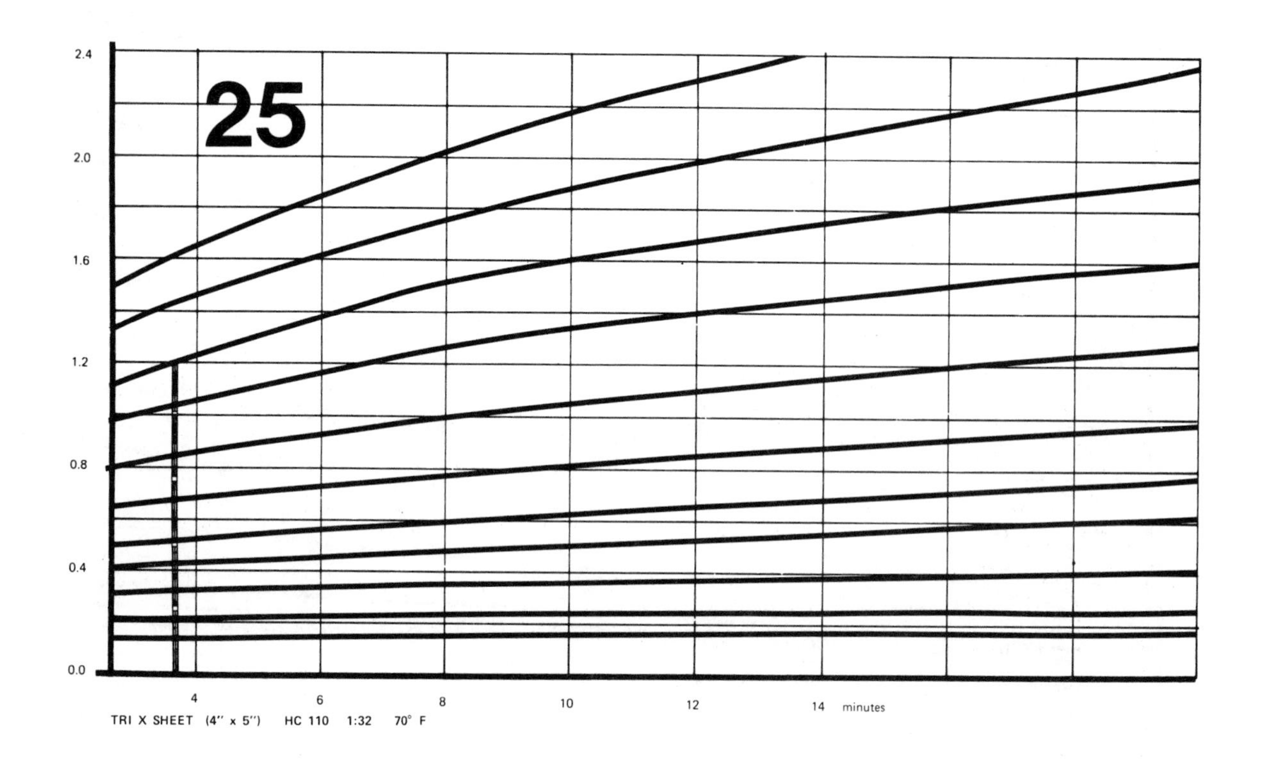
25
2.4
2.0
1.6
1.2
0.8
0.4
0.0
4
6
8
10
12
14 minutes
TRI X SHEET (4" x 5") HC 110 1:32 70° F

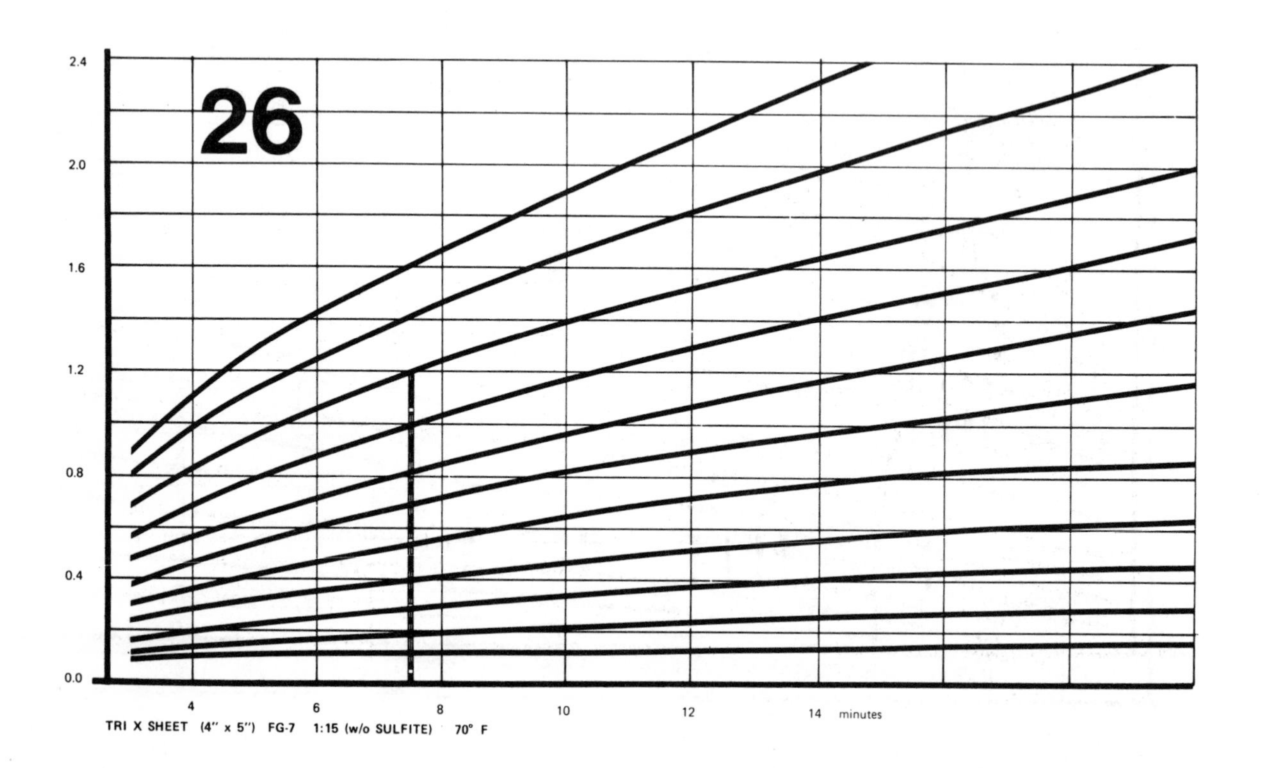
26
2.4
2.0
1.6
1.2
0.8
0.4
0.0
4
6
8
10
12
14 minutes
TRI X SHEET (4" x 5") FG-7 1:15 (w/o SULFITE) 70° F

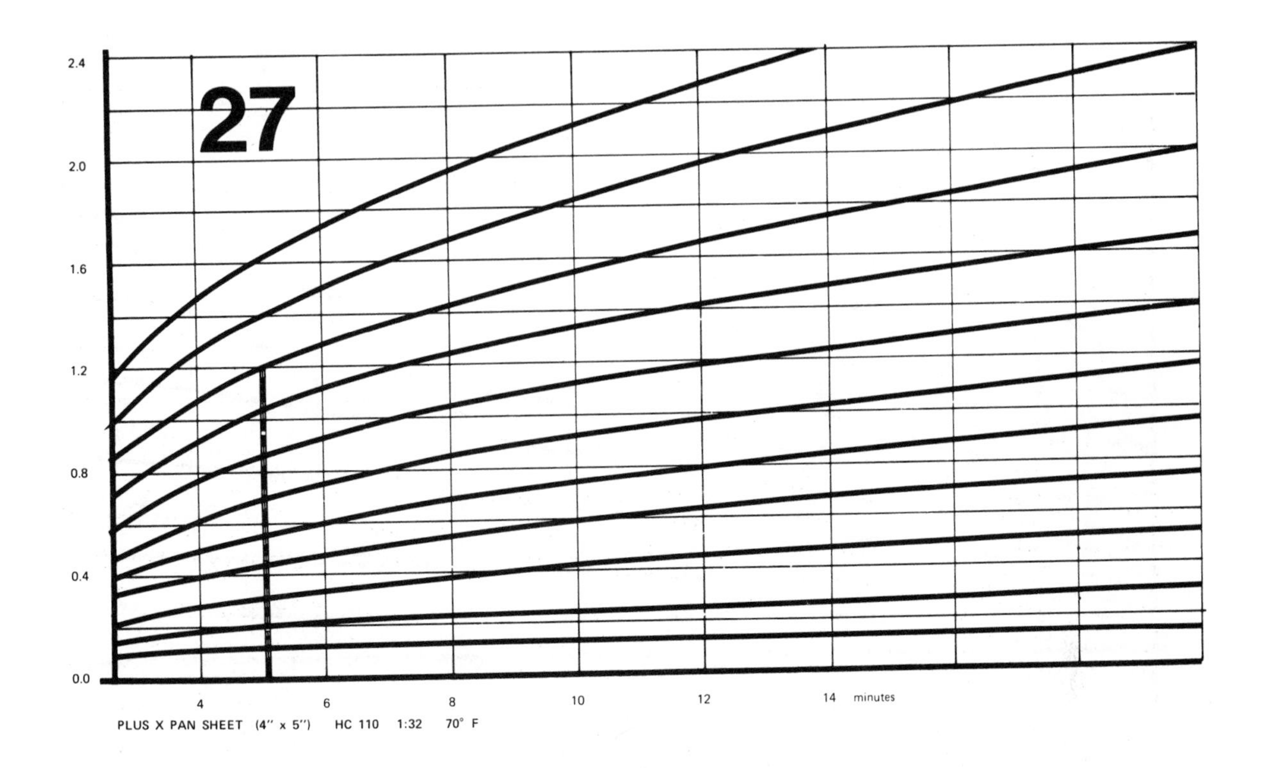
27
2.4
2.0
1.6
1.2
0.8
0.4
0.0
4
6
8
10
12
14 minutes
PLUS X PAN SHEET (4" x 5") HC 110 1:32 70° F

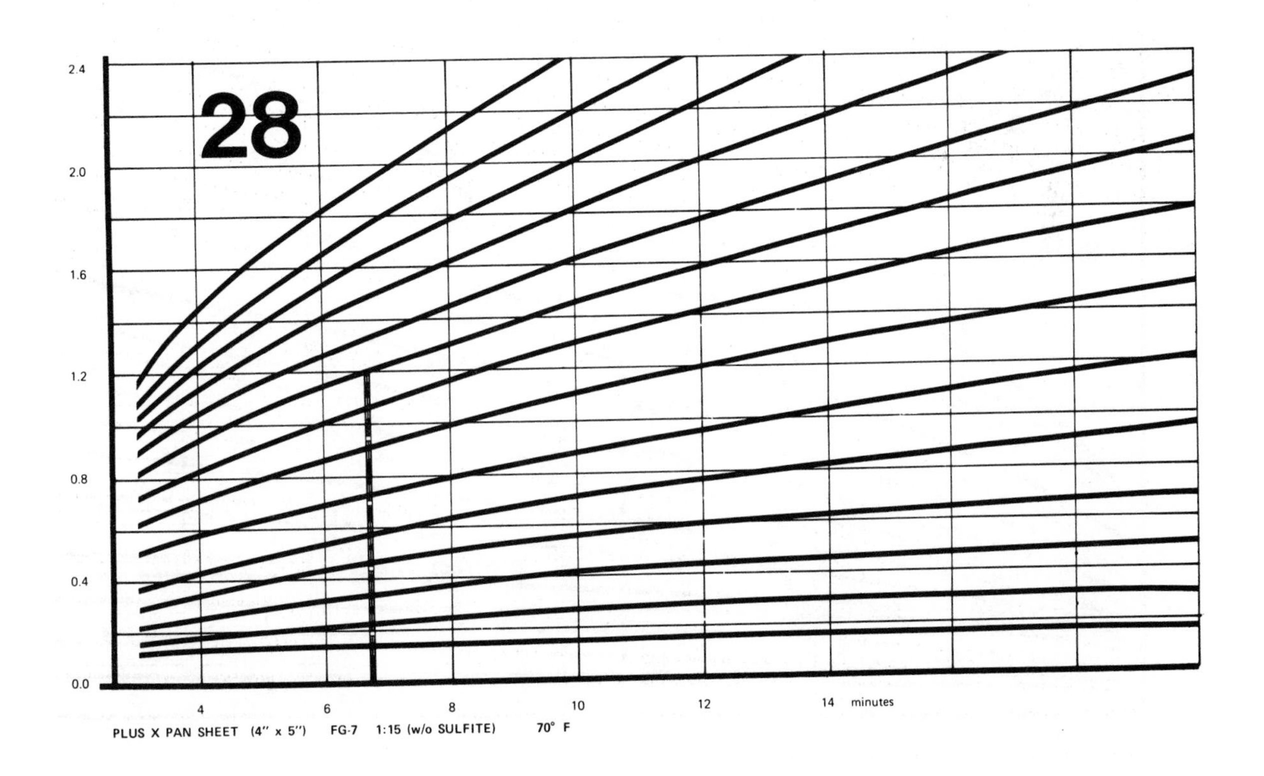
28
2.4
2.0
1.6
1.2
0.8
0.4
0.0
4
6
8
10
12
14 minutes
PLUS X PAN SHEET (4" x 5") FG-7 1:15 (w/o SULFITE) 70° F

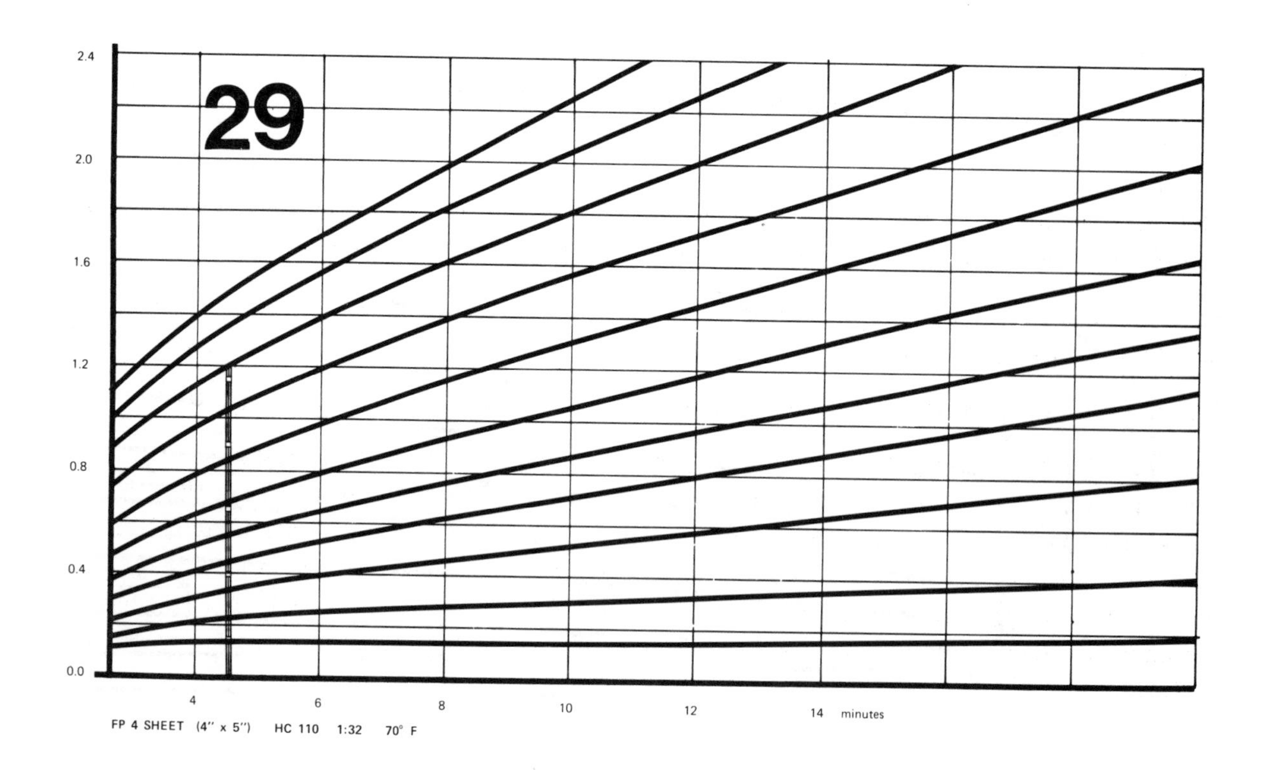

29
2.4
2.0
1.6
1.2
0.8
0.4
0.0
4
6
8
10
12
14 minutes
FP 4 SHEET (4" x 5") HC 110 1:32 70° F

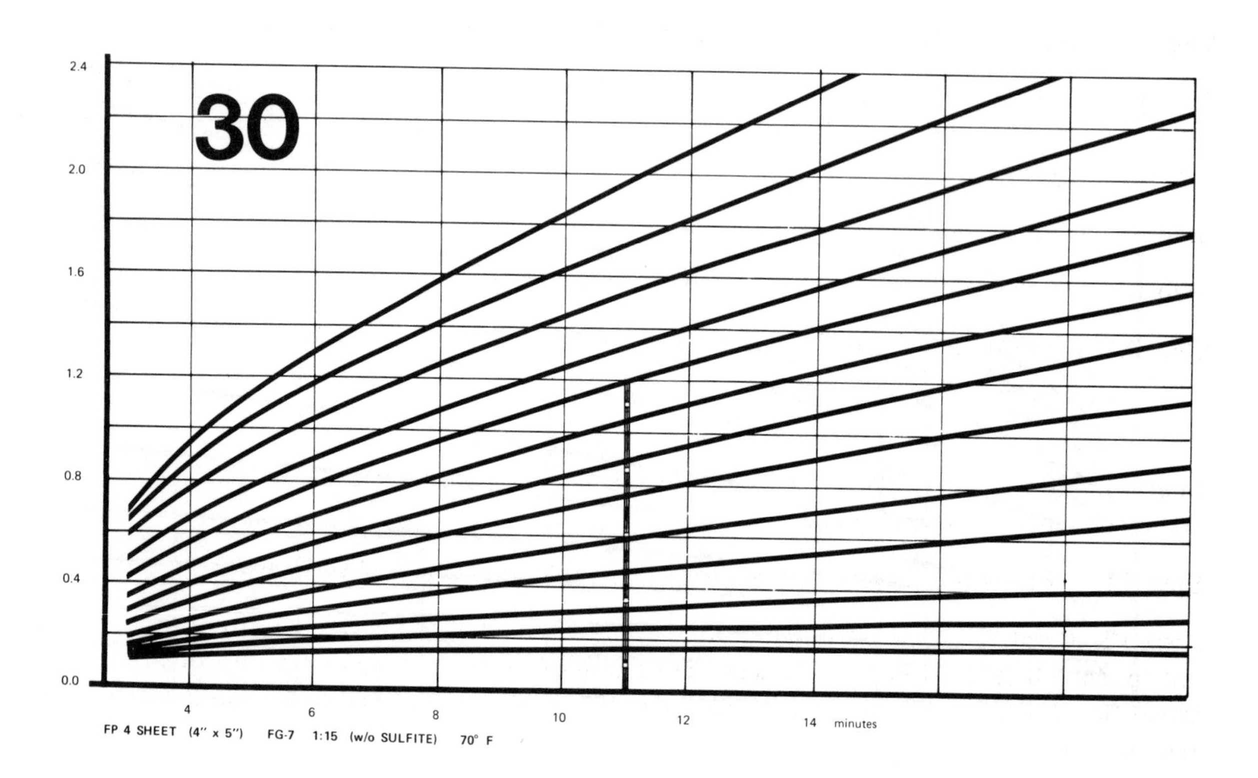

30
2.4
2.0
1.6
1.2
0.8
0.4
0.0
4
6
8
10
12
14 minutes
FP 4 SHEET (4" x 5") FG-7 1:15 (w/o SULFITE) 70° F

DEVELOPER—DENSITY PARAMETERS

Step 1. Set up a greycard target in an even light. Use the Manufacturer's Index. Calculate an exposure for normal placement of the greycard. Record it for reference.

Step 2. Expose the first frame five *f*-numbers less than the indicated exposure. This will place the exposure on Zone 0.

Step 3. Expose the second frame four *f*-numbers less than the indicated exposure.

Step 4. Continue this pattern, exposing each subsequent frame one *f*-number more than the preceding frame. Do this for ten frames total. Attempt to keep the exposures in the middle range of shutter speeds. Very high speeds are often in error on small cameras. Use the speeds of 1/30th through 1/250th of a second. Light the greycard so the first exposure is 1/125 of a second at *f*-16 and all the other exposures will be easy to accomplish. It is better to change the aperture than the shutter in these tests, since there is usually less error (camera to camera) in the apertures.

Step 5. Repeat the first four steps, exposing three additional rolls of film.

Step 6. Develop Roll 1 for 1/2X the time suggested by the manufacturer of the film. If you are using a film in a developer for which there are no reference times, use the time for another film of similar speed.

Step 7. Develop Roll 2 for the suggested time.

Step 8. Develop Roll 3 for 1¾X of the suggested time.

Step 9. Develop Roll 4 for 2½X the suggested time.

Step 10. After the film has been fixed, washed, and dried, measure the densities for each roll and record them, frame by frame.

Step 11. Plot density in vertical rows for each development time. See Figure 3-1.

Step 12. Connect all the bottom densities. These show what happens to an exposure equivalent to Zone 0 as development changes. Do the same for the density points for Zone I, II, etc. When finished the graph should look like the parametric curves of Figure 3-3 and the following figures.

USING THE DEVELOPER–DENSITY PARAMETRIC CURVES

As a result of the tests made for Standard Exposure Time and those for Normal Development you have negatives that print normally for your system. If 35-mm negatives are used, the normal highlight density will be about 1.15. If larger format negatives are used, the density will be about 1.30.

Using the densitometer, measure the highest textured highlight areas on several good negatives. Average these densities. Draw a horizontal line on your parametric graph at this density (see the sample graphs on following pages). Find the place where this line intersects the Zone VIII curve. From the intersection of these two drop a vertical line to the bottom of the graph. Read off the development time in minutes. This is the Normal Time for the film and developer combination you have tested.

To determine a one-Zone expansion (N+) development time, find where the highest textured highlight density line crosses the Zone VII curve. Drop a vertical line from this point; read the developing time in minutes. This will be some time longer than normal. This is called the Normal Plus development. It is used to compensate for a slightly flat scene.

To determine development time for a moderately contrasty scene, one that requires compression of densities in the negative, find where the highest textured highlight density intersects the Zone IX curve. Draw a vertical line from this intersection down to the base (something less than the Normal time). This is the time required to compress the negative densities that would result from a long-scale scene so that they will print on normal contrast grade paper. It is called a Normal Minus (N–) development.

The parametric curves are useful for economically examining film and developer combinations. They are not magical; their effectiveness is limited if used only to determine development times.

It is important to realize that curves made from a single set of tests will not be absolutely smooth when the information is first plotted on the graph paper. The sample curves are idealized or "smoothed" curves. They are not presented as absolutes but as guides. They are typical results of student work.

An engineer making these tests would expose a larger number of rolls or sheets of film. The results of these many sets of information would be statistically averaged. These average densities would be plotted. A neater set of curves would result. In making an economical set of personal working curves some approximations must be made.

The easiest way to draw the curves from a single set of density figures is by using a plastic "irregular curve". The DIETZGEN 2152-21 is suitable. It is shaped rather like the outline of an Indian club, knobby at one end, and with a long smooth "handle". The shape of this plastic guide fits directly the majority of density curves encountered.

Place the plastic curve on the graph paper so that the lowest density and the highest density points for a middle Zone lie on the curve. Slide the curve to the left or right until the plotted densities bracket it (study the sample graph on page 52). When the density points lie smoothly on either side, or fall on the curved line formed by the guide, draw a line lightly with a hard pencil.

Move the curve up to the next set of data points. The plastic guide will probably fit directly if it is slid a little to the right. Each higher set of points will have a steeper slope (for the shortening development times) and then flatten out toward the horizontal as the developing times increase.

For the Zone lines below Zone V, the curve will slide a little to the left for each lower Zone line. Near the "handle" of the plastic curve the line becomes more and more nearly straight.

Sketch all the curves in lightly; stand back and examine the whole set. They should have a smooth even appearance. Large gaps between lines or sharp angular bends are cause for suspicion. A density that falls too far outside the smooth curve may have to be ignored. The reasons for this are many. For example, accidents of exposing, processing, or measuring.

A good graph paper to use for the parametrics is supplied in pads by K&E: Albanene Guide Line Prepared Tracing Paper No. 10-5645. It has a grid of inch-square lines divided into tenth of inch grids. The lines are printed in light blue. They are easy to see but do not dominate. Some graph papers have dark green lines; a graph drawn on this paper is difficult to read.

A set of homemade parametric curves are summations of the average forces working on the film: meter, shutter, light, temperature, film emulsion, developer, agitation, and yourself, as operator of the system. One photographer will make a set of parametrics which will not exactly fit another photographer's working system. Note that even within the *Handbook* there are apparent inconsistencies as a result of this. For example, Normal developing time for Plus X Pan in the Standard Method Development is different from that found in the parametric curves. The Standard Method time includes a contrast-reducing safety factor.

Figure 3-1 illustrates the three important areas of the typical parametric curve. Area *a* is to the left of the normal time line. Area *b* to the right and above Zone V. Area *c* is to the right and below Zone V.

AREA *A*: TIME LESS THAN NORMAL DEVELOPMENT

The shape of the parametric curves to the left of the Normal time line tells how useful the film will be for compression development. Compare the curves in this area. Examples to study are for PLUS-X PAN developed in D-76 and the same film developed in RODINAL (shown in the sample graphs).

Find the place where the Normal time line intersects the 1.20 density line (note: actual working highlight density will vary between 1.15 and 1.30 in most cases. The 1.20 density line has been chosen for this discussion as a working compromise). Follow to the left along the 1.20 density line. On the D-76 set of curves there are two Zone lines that cross (IX and X). In this useful range of developing times it is possible to achieve easily and repeatably two Zones of compression. Compare this with the Rodinal curves. Look to the left along the 1.20 density line from Normal time: three Zone curves cross. This indicates the developer has a compression usefulness greater than that of the other developer.

The area between zero developing time and one-half Normal is not useful for quality development. The film has been wetted too short a time for the complex physical processes of development to have predictability.

AREA *B*: TIME GREATER THAN NORMAL DEVELOPMENT

(ZONES V through VII)

Increasing development time increases density range. What the parametrics do not show are the other changes in the film, notably the increase in grain size and apparent loss of image sharpness (or acuity) as a result of processing effects on the silver in the emulsion.

All processing must eventually be evaluated in the print.

A 2½ times increase in development time is about the maximum that can be used with a medium-sized negative and still achieve smooth results (at four to five diameters enlargement). With a small negative even less development can be tolerated if an illusionistic rendering of smooth surfaces is desired. If the granularity of the film is desired as an esthetic device, development can be extended even further.

A developer with little silver solvent will generally produce a more sharply granular image than one containing large quantities of sulfite or thiocyanate. Compare Rodinal with D-76 to verify this.

Examine the parametric curves for D-76. Follow the 1.20 density line to the right from normal time. Note that at 2½ times the Normal time, the Zone V line almost intersects the 1.20 density line. It is possible to achieve about three Zones of expansion but the parametric tells nothing about image granularity.

Compare the Rodinal parametrics with the D-76 curves. On the Rodinal curve the same degree of expansion can be achieved by doubling development time. The preference for one developer over another depends on the quality of the resulting negative.

AREA *C*: TIMES GREATER THAN NORMAL DEVELOPMENT

(ZONES O through V)

The low Zones of the negative have little density even with extended development. This can be verified by examining the changes of the 0, I, II, and even the Zone III density lines. The fact that the densities of the low Zones change little is of importance. Ansel Adams noted that the Zone System is predicated on this fact: increasing development time causes large increases in highlight density; increasing development time creates little more shadow density.

Highlight density control is achieved with ease; there is a direct relationship between development time and high Zone densities. Shadow separation control is more difficult; it is dependent both on the characteristics of a film and on the developer used.

Examine the parametric curve in Figure 3-2. The Zone lines for 0, I, II, and III are close together; they remain essentially parallel throughout the usable range of developing time. The parametric curves predict that Zones below IV would be crushed together. If major areas of a picture require good separation of Zones II, III, and IV, then the negative exposure must be increased. Placing the subject one Zone higher (as can be seen on the parametric curves) results in separation of tones. Using a developer that produces more vigorous separations of low tones will also provide more definite rendering of shadow areas. A different film might be used. Note the separation of low Zones provided by Plus-X Pan compared to Tri-X.

Another example is found in the comparison offered on the charts for ILFORD FP-4 developed in FG-7 and D-76. Note that FG-7 produces greater overall shadow densities and more separation of low Zones; the same film with D-76 has less shadow separation.

Verify the kind of silver image a film and developer combination produces by printing. Decide if it is useful esthetically. The parametric curves permit anticipating controls and predicting tonal relationships for a developer and film.

SYSTEM INDEX DETERMINATION FROM THE PARAMETRIC CURVE

An accurate System Index for a new film and developer combination need not be determined by trial-and-error before making exposure and development tests for parametric curves. The tests incorporate Index information.

Make the exposure tests for the parametrics, develop the film and plot the curves. Note the separation between what has been arbitrarily called the Zone 0 line and the Zone I line. If the System Index used was accurate, these two lines will have a density difference of 0.03 to 0.06. This is for 35-mm film. For a larger format film the difference will be 0.10 to 0.15. These densities are at Normal developing time.

If the space between the lines is greater than that, assume the System Index was numerically low and the film overexposed. The graph lines can be renamed. Zone I becomes Zone II, etc. If there is essentially no distance between lines, the System Index was too high. It should be lowered and the graph lines renamed. Zone II becomes Zone I, etc.

PARAMETRIC TESTING WITH SHEET FILM

Using one sheet of film for each test exposure will yield the most accurate information but three exposures can be made on each sheet of film to reduce costs. This will create a small error. This error can be anticipated and allowed for. The Clayden effect will change the spacing of the parametric curves. A second exposure onto a piece of film identical in quantity to the first will not cause a doubling of the density. The second exposure will have less effect than it ought to have. The error is not great but may be noticeable.

Set up a Grey Card target. Calculate an exposure for Zone I placement. Remove the dark slide completely and expose for Zone I (see Figure 3-2). Push the dark slide in one-third of the way and expose the sheet again *for the same exposure*. Push the dark slide in two-thirds and expose the film a third time, increasing the exposure a full stop (see Figure 3-2).

Continue the series by placing a new film holder in the camera. Expose a whole sheet for a Zone IV. Continue exposing the sheet in thirds. The Sample Exposure Table with Figure 3-2 provides a sample description of exposures for four sheets of film.

When the four sheets are developed together they will provide one column of information for the parametric curves. Three sets, or 12 sheets, will outline a total set of parametric curves. Four sets will provide more information.

If all the exposures on a piece of film added uniformly, the three areas would have equal density separations on the parametric graphs. Because of the Clayden effect (see Todd and Zakia: *Photographic Densitometry*. Morgan and Morgan) the densities on each sheet of film will cluster. The first exposure will show a "correct" density. The next two will each affect the film slightly less than one would predict. The result is that the parametric curves will appear in groups of three.

Using only three exposures to a sheet, the error is not out of bounds. The lowest line of each cluster is accurate. The error in the others can be estimated visually and the spaces between lines evened out after they have been plotted initially.

ADVANCED PRINTING CONTROLS

Zone Controls will produce a more carefully exposed and developed negative. The ultimate purpose of these is a better representation of the image. There also are precise controls for the print.

Each combination of paper, developer, and darkroom equipment will affect the image.

> *By making tests you may discover the minimum and maximum developing times to produce black print tones and yet not degrade the highlight values.*
>
> *Investigate the practical modifications of the paper developers. They become usable tools.*
>
> *Variations caused by changing development time and developer dilutions must be examined so changes in the image are understood.*
>
> *Most contemporary paper developers have two active agents in them that cause the silver image to become visible. One is very sensitive to lowered working temperature (Hydroquinone) and is also the agent that tends to produce contrast in the image. Permitting the developer to cool much below 70° inhibits this agent.*

Minimum development: It is useful to know the shortest time you can develop a properly exposed piece of paper to produce a "maximum black". Photographic paper responds the way film does to development. If time is increased the heavily exposed portions of the picture tend to darken proportionally more than light areas. Decreased developing time shortens the tonal range. There is a limiting condition: no matter how fully the print is exposed, maximum black areas cannot achieve full visual density with less than a certain amount of development.

a. Expose a test patch of paper under the enlarger. Make a Standard Black Patch. This maximum black is for this particular combination of paper and developer. Maintain the developer at a temperature between 70 and 75 degrees.

b. Cut a sheet of 8×10 inch normal contrast grade paper into quarters (American 2; Agfa 3). Expose under the enlarger as you did when making the Standard Black Patch.

c. Mark the pieces 20″, 40″, 60″ and 80″; develop them for the length of time noted. Transfer them to the stop bath without draining.

d. Fix and dry these patches.

e. When the patches are dry compare them with a Standard Black Patch. The test with the shortest developing time that compares favorably with the Standard Black Patch is the Minimum Development Time. The next shorter developing time will definitely be more grey. Record this time.

Maximum development: To produce a print with the longest possible grey scale it is necessary to push all materials and controls to useful limits. Increased development time changes the tonal range. Darks get darker without the pale grey tones darkening...to a point. Discover where this point occurs. How long can one develop a print, producing richer blacks but not degrading the highlights?

Reducing agents in developers will eventually reduce silver salts to visible densities whether exposed to light or not. Extended development will also do this. It can be prevented. Keep developing time within safe limits or chemically modify the developer by increasing the inhibitor.

a. Cut an 8×10 inch sheet of paper into fourths. Expose each of these pieces to produce a Zone VII value. Try 5 seconds at *f*-22 or *f*-32. The idea is to make a light tone to compare with the white of the paper. Determine such an exposure, then expose identically four test patches but cover half of each with a piece of black paper.

b. Develop the patches for 2, 3, 5, and 7 minutes under your normal darkroom conditions.

c. Repeat the same test but develop in total darkness. This is a control set. Develop a fresh patch cut from paper never exposed to any light. This is the whitest white you can obtain from the paper you are using. The emulsion itself is grey and will never be as white as the paper that supports it.

d. Compare these patches when dry. Look for yellow stains, and dirty grey areas in the "white" paper. The longest developing time without color changes is the maximum developing time possible.

CHARACTERISTICS OF PAPER DEVELOPERS

A developer is a mixture of different chemicals that work in harmony to make visible the latent photographic image. Small changes of proportions produce different effects. The mixtures sold under proprietary names (for example, Dektol, Vividol, Printofine) are stable and dependable. They will last a long time in the tray. They store well in bottles and remain stable and useful for weeks.

The basic components of developers are:

1. *Reducing agent.* The ingredient that causes the image to become visible. The exposed silver is reduced from a salt to a metal. Most contemporary developers use two reducers, with complementary characteristics. These are Elon or Metol (both are proprietary names) and Hydroquinone. Elon produces a low contrast image and can cause an overall fogging (greyness) with increased development. This is prevented by the addition of a restrainer or inhibitor. The color of the image is affected by the reducing agent. Elon produces a neutral black image.

   Hydroquinone is a high contrast reducing agent. It is not as active as Elon and it does not work well at low temperatures. Below 60 degrees it does not work at all. At higher temperatures it is more effective, proportionately, than Elon. The image it produces is brownish-black.

2. *Preservative.* The primary purpose of the preservative is to remove free oxygen from the developing solution. Free oxygen destroys the reducing agent. The preservative also adds some alkalinity. Most reducing agents require an alkaline solution. The most commonly used preservative is Sodium Sulfite.

3. *Accelerator.* The reducing agent by itself is weak and must be activated by an accelerator. The accelerator is an alkaline chemical and sodium carbonate is most commonly used in film and paper developers. For strong solutions this is supplemented or replaced with Sodium Hydroxide.

4. *Restrainer.* The reducing agent eventually develops silver in the emulsion whether or not it has been exposed. Only by restraining its activity can an overall greyness be avoided. Restrainers actually prevent development but make controlled development possible, as auto brakes permit control of a car. Restrainers also change the color of the silver image. The most common restrainer is Potassium Bromide. Bromide makes the image greenish-black. Other restrainers produce different colors. DUPONT "B-B" solution preserves the blue-black tone of contemporary enlarging papers. KODAK Anti-Fog No. 1 is used in place of Bromide in some formulas and also preserves the original silver image color. Restrainers change the contrast of the image. Increasing the amount of the restrainer increases contrast.

5. *Solvent.* Chemicals are dissolved in a solvent so they may interact and can be carried into the emulsion of the film or paper. Water is the usual solvent and tap water is usually adequate. Distilled or de-ionized water is needed for some special formulas. When water is mentioned in the *Handbook*, tap water is meant unless otherwise noted.

EXPERIMENTAL INTRODUCTION TO DEVELOPERS

1. Using a negative that "prints well" without needing dodging or burning, make a 5x8 inch print. Develop this in a standard paper developer for a standard time. Note the enlarger lens setting, the exposure time, and the development time and temperature.

Expose eight prints identical to the first. Store them in a light-safe place for testing.

2. Take two clean print processing trays and place one liter of water at 75 degrees F in each tray.

3.	**LEFT TRAY**	**RIGHT TRAY**
	Stir in one-half teaspoonful of Hydroquinone	*Stir in one-half teaspoonful of Hydroquinone*

3a. Mark two of the exposed prints 3L and 3R and develop each in its correct tray for the time noted in Step 1. After developing the prints complete processing through fixing them.

4.	*Stir in a heaping tablespoon of Sodium Sulfite*	*Stir in a heaping tablespoon of Sodium Sulfite*

4a. Mark, and then develop two more of the exposed prints, one in each of the trays, for the time determined in Step 1. After development, stop them and fix them normally.

5.	*Stir in a teaspoon of Sodium Carbonate*	*Stir in a teaspoon of Sodium Carbonate*

5a. Mark and develop and fix two more prints.

6.	*Stir in one-eighth of a teaspoon of Potassium Bromide*	*Stir in one-eighth of a teaspoon of Potassium Bromide*

6a. Develop and fix the last two of the pre-exposed prints from Step 1.

7. When all the prints are fixed, neutralize, wash and dry them.Study them and compare to learn what has happened at each stage of the experiment. Observe the comparative energy of the Hydroquinone as compared to the Elon, both without and with the Sodium Carbonate.

Observe the changes in contrast (clarity of whites and separation of tones overall) first without and then with the Potassium Bromide (added in Step 6).

COMPOUNDING DEVELOPERS

Developers can be mixed from separate ingredients. This takes time but is less expensive than purchasing premixed chemicals. A scale is needed to weigh the chemicals accurately. Student grade triple-beam balances are available from $30.00. Certain formulas listed in the *Handbook* are not manufactured and must be mixed. All the work in Reversal Processing and Non-silver

Processes require compounding and mixing chemicals.

Common developer formulas are listed below. On the left are paper developers, on the right are film developers. The Beers formula is an excellent developer.

Mix the chemicals in the order listed. Water should be 90 to 120 degrees. If it is hotter some of the chemicals will decompose. If colder, some will not dissolve easily. The Hydroquinone stock does not keep well. Do not mix more than can be used in two weeks and store in a cool place.

COMMON DEVELOPERS[1]

	Paper Developers		Beers Formulas		Film Developers		
Chemical[2]	D-72[3]	54-D[4]	A	B	D-23[5]	D-76[6]	Notes
Metol	12.4	10.8	16.0		30.0	8.0	
Sodium sulfite	180.0	160.0	46.0	46.0	400.0	400.0	dessicated = anhydrous
Hydroquinone	48.0	42.4		16.0		20.0	
Sodium carbonate	320.0	352.0	47.0	63.0			'monohydrate'
Borax						8.0	
Potassium bromide	76 ml	32 ml	22 ml	44 ml			10% stock solution
Water	4 liters	4 liters	2 liters (see table below)	2 liters	4 liters	4 liters	start with 2½ liters; mix all chemicals and add water to final total volume.

1. Data from the *Basic Photo Series* and the *Photo Lab Index.*
2. All weights are in grams
3. D-72 is the same as Dektol.
4. 54-D is a cold tone developer that works well with Agfa papers, producing tones without a blue cast.
5. D-23 is a very soft working film developer most suitable for harsh lighting.
6. D-76 is a standard fine-grain developer.

BEERS FORMULA DILUTION TABLE[1]

	Contrast						
	Low	2	3	Medium	5	6	High
"A"	16	14	12	10	8	6	4 ounces
"B"	0	2	4	6	8	10	28 ounces
Water	16	16	16	16	16	16	0 ounces

1. To produce approximately a full grade of contrast control with a single developer and paper grade.

Because Metinol U is not generally available in this country, various alternatives have been sought. The following formula seems to be a close substitute. Its origin is obscure and it might be thought of as an "underground" equivalent of the Agfa developer.

Chemical	Quantity (liters or grams)	
Water	¾	3
Metol (Elon)	1	4
Sodium Sulfite (dess.)	13	52
Hydroquinone	3	12
Sodium Carbonate (mono.)	30	120
Potassium Bromide	1	4
Water to make	1	4

MODIFYING PAPER DEVELOPERS

Prepackaged developers are usually adequate but there are times when it is desirable to modify them. Developers may be modified to change contrast or to change image color. Diluting the developer reduces contrast.

Contrast can be increased by reducing the dilution, increasing the amount of restrainer, or increasing Hydroquinone. The last two methods also change image color.

The characteristic color of the image is controlled by the size of silver particles formed during development. The smaller silver particles are seen as reddish-brown. The coarsest image is blue-black. Increasing the Bromide makes the image greenish-black. These descriptive terms are comparative; experience in viewing different papers is needed before they have meaning.

Increasing Hydroquinone to increase contrast. Adding Hydroquinone to a developer that already has Elon in it increases contrast. It increases separation in the lower Zones.

Examine the Beers Developer formulas (see *Basic Photo Series*, Volume 3, p. 114) and the Common Developers Table. A change of a full paper contrast grade is a change in the ratio of Hydroquinone to Elon of about 7:1. A soft-working developer has equal amounts of Elon and Hydroquinone. A high-contrast developer has about seven times as much Hydroquinone.

Moderate shifts of contrast can be obtained by using a Hydroquinone stock made by dissolving 3 grams of Hydroquinone in 8 ounces of water. Add 10 grams of Sodium Sulfite to preserve it. This stock solution is added to a working developer.

To increase contrast add two ounces of the Hydroquinone stock to a normal working tray of developer. Develop a print in this developer and compare it with a print developed in standard developer. Note the change in contrast and color. The change will be mostly in Zones 0 to IV.

For a detailed examination make grey-patch strips. Expose 3 inch strips of paper to light in one-inch increments. Expose each inch of paper one second more than the preceding inch. Exposures range from 1 second to 10 seconds at *f*-8. Develop one strip in standard developer at normal dilution. Develop the second strip in developer with 2 ounces of Hydroquinone stock. The third strip may be developed in enriched developer with 4 ounces. Compare the tests.

SELENIUM TONING FOR IMAGE INTENSIFICATION

Slight changes in image color caused by changing developers or modifying developers can be overcome by toning. Mild selenium toning also intensifies the image. The selenium metal is linked to the silver image. The more silver in the print the more selenium is deposited. Where there is no silver (in the white areas) there is no color change. A mild tone intensifies the print, making the blacks blacker and not changing whites at all.

Wet the prints prepared for toning. These prints are otherwise complete and ready for mounting. While they are soaking prepare a bath consisting of one cup of Sodium Thiosulfate crystals dissolved in one quart of lukewarm water.

Also prepare a bath of hypo eliminating solution and selenium toner. Use fresh eliminator. The solution will stain if it has been used for clearing other prints. To one quart of working strength hypo eliminating solution add 25 ml of KODAK Rapid Selenium Toner (or GAF Flemish Toner). This solution is for American papers. For Agfa papers add 50 ml of toner to the hypo eliminating solution. The toning solution is used between 75 and 80 degrees.

Fix the wet prints in plain thiosulfate for five minutes. Drain them; do not allow them to be wetted with plain water. Place them in the toning bath one at a time. Do not tone more than eight prints in a quart of toning solution. Agitate the prints constantly by pulling the bottom print free and laying it on top.

The selenium will change the color of the black and near-black areas of the print. The change is mild because the toning solution is weak. Place an untoned wet print beside the tray with the prints being toned. Compare it to the prints in the toning solution. After about five minutes there will be a perceptible strengthening of blacks. Allow the toning to continue for another 30 to 40 seconds and then place the prints in a wash tray. Dump the toner.

Put the prints in a fresh solution of hypo eliminator for the length of time suggested by the manufacturer. Agitate them constantly. Return them to the washing tray for 20 minutes and then dry them on racks or towels.

MOUNTING, FINISHING, AND STORING PRINTS

A print is difficult to see until it is mounted or held flat under glass. The surface of a silver print is highly reflective and if it is bent it reflects the general room lights into a viewer's eyes, distracting him from the print.

Mounting also changes a photographer's understanding of his image. Mounting a photograph produces a new "psychic distance" for the photographer and allows him to see the picture in a new way.

There is probably no simpler way to hold prints flat than to dry mount them. There are two types of dry mounting tissue on the market. One is a sheet of glossy material that melts into the back of the print and the surface of the cardboard when heated to about 170 degrees. The other melts at a lower temperature; it is a waxy substance coated on a thin paper support. The KODAK Dry Mount Tissue is sold in packages of 25 and 150 sheets. It is safe to use for normal papers; some color print papers and the softer warmtone papers can be marred at the temperatures needed to fuse it.

When mounting prints place a clean piece of mounting board and a cover sheet, used to protect the surface of the print, into the press and close it. Allow them to heat for 20 seconds. This will drive out excess moisture—a necessity in all damp climates. Dry out each sheet of board before using it. This prevents bubbles from forming. These often do not appear at first but become apparent later.

The size of the mounting board is important. The location of the print on the board also affects the response.

There are different degrees of quality mount boards. There are fewer colors and types on the market now than a few years ago. Cheap boards are suitable for proof or study prints. Student-grade bristol board is often used. This has thin cover paper over a filler of grey chip board. Intermediate grades of board have a bleached filler. The most expensive and the most permanent boards are made of rag; no wood pulp is in either the cover or the filler. The only 100% rag board in this country are BAINBRIDGE (Museum Board) and CRESCENT PAPER (No. 1155). These boards cost 2 to 5 times as much as the matt boards sold in most art supply houses. They will not "fox", i.e., discolor with age, and they will not cause destruction of the silver image. The best general purpose board of medium quality is STRATHMORE Illustration Board. This is supplied in two thicknesses.

Prints up to 8×10 inches may be "center mounted"—placed in the exact center of the board. Visual tension results from such placement. Larger prints need extra space at the bottom of the board, otherwise the lower margin appears smaller than it actually is.

For the safety of the print, and to isolate the print from the world, the smallest mount size should be about 8×10 inches. Prints up to 5×7 inches may be mounted on 11×14 inch boards. The smallest board for 8×10 inch prints should be about 14×16 inches.

An exception to this is some prints profit by being mounted with no margins whatever. Photographers borrow a term from the printing trade (where an image is printed so as to "bleed" off the edge of the paper, where it is trimmed away) and call a print "bleed mounted" when it is trimmed to the edge of the image, leaving no margin.

Overmatting means cutting a neat hole in a piece of suitable board and placing the print behind the matt. Another piece of board completes the matt, protecting the back of the print. The two pieces are hinged together with brown butchers tape. Pressure-sensitive tape should not be used because the adhesive is not permanent and will eventually decay.

A matt can be cut easily with a DEXTER Matt-cutter. This tool holds a blade at an angle. It costs about $5.00. The Matt-cutter is pushed along the outline of the opening desired; working from the back side of the matt. A neat cut can be made if the matt board is supported on two strips of board so the blade of the cutter passes between them but does not drag underneath. Dragging the tip of the blade causes the cutter to wave. The Dexter cutter is comfortable only for right-handed persons. A larger cutter made by EXACTO can be used by left-handed artists. It costs about $15.00.

Do not allow one print to slide on another. The gelatin surface is frail. Protect the print with a cover sheet of a firm paper, or overmatt it. When handling a print never place thumbs on them; finger oils will be imprinted and dirt will cling to them, smudging the matt.

A fine print represents several hours of work, often spread out over a period of several days. Protect this investment. Storage boxes can be purchased or made. A good way to store prints is in boxes with strips of polyfoam sold to upholster cushions. These strips will protect corners.

The print may need spotting. Dust on the negative makes white spots on the print. Cover these with dye. SPOTONE dyes are available in sets of three colors. Mixing these allows any color of print emulsion to be matched. Dyes are applied with a fine brush. The best is the WINDSOR AND NEWTON Series 7, Size 00.

Shake the bottle of dye, remove the cap, and then work out of the cap. Set the bottle itself to one side where it cannot be knocked over. Spot large dust spots from the center, speckling the area and working out toward the edges. Do not overspot.

REVERSAL PROCESSING OF FILMS

Black and white transparencies (also called diapositives) have many uses. They are an alternative solution to prints for displays and exhibitions and present creative possibilities that could not have been anticipated before the cassette tape recorder and pulse-actuated automatic slide projector.

Any black and white film can be processed to a positive. Slides can be made from negatives if desired by printing onto KODAK Fine Grain Positive film. The black tones of the Fine Grain Positive can be enriched by careful toning with KODAK Selenium Toner (see Step No. 10, Reversal Processing for Copying Prints). This requires making a negative and then a film print.

Copying prints for lectures is economical and straightforward with the following chemistry. The Kodak process for Direct Positive Film (DP-402) has been modified to increase the contrast and produce higher maximum density without significantly increasing grain size. This produces slides that are "projection equivalents" of the original prints. The chemical compounds noted are designed to produce a slide that will provide a projected image ranging from apparent black to clear film in an auditorium seating 200.

Standard KODAK Carousel projectors are assumed. Denser blacks can be produced by increasing the Sodium Hydroxide as much as 20%; decreasing it proportionately creates softer tones.

Reversal processing produces a conventional negative; instead of removing the unused silver, the silver metal image is etched away. After the negative image has been "bleached" the remaining silver is exposed and developed. If the negative was properly exposed the complimentary image produced will be a full scale positive.

Because the negative and positive images are physical complements to one another, contrast control cannot be accomplished by increasing or decreasing the development time. To do so destroys one portion of the image or another. Increasing or decreasing the activity of the developer changes the tonal range to use the entire silver density range desired. These controls are straightforward. Sodium Hydroxide is the principal accelerator and Hydroquinone is the most effective contrast controlling reducing agent. Changing the proportions of these stocks in the developer will change the contrast. Increasing the Hydroxide increases contrast. Increasing Hydroquinone increases (and to some degree harshens) the separation of low tones.

These processes are suitable for sheet films. Some experimentation is always necessary with a reversal process to determine accurate system indexes. Expose by metering the important textured *highlights* in the subject; place exposures at Zone VII. Meter and then expose two *f*-stops more than the indicated exposure.

REVERSAL PROCESSING FOR COPYING PRINTS

For processing KODAK DP-5246, DP-402 or Panatomic-X; approximately 30 rolls (36 exposure) may be processed in each gallon of solution (excepting toning bath).

First Developer: (D-19[1] modified[2])

Water (125°F)	3	liters
Elon	8	gram
Sodium Sulfite (desc.)	360	gram
Hydroquinone	32	gram
Sodium Carbonate (mono.)	220	gram
[2]*Sodium Thiocyanate*	*8*	*gram*
[2]*Sodium Hydroxide* . . . . *2-10 gram,* *normal for copying prints*	*5*	*gram*
Potassium Bromide	20	gram

[1]*The published variations in the D-19 formula have offered these differences: Metol, 8–8.8 grams, Sodium Sulfite, 360–400 grams; Hydroquinone, 32–34.2 grams; Carbonate, 188–220 grams.*

Bleach

Water (125° *F* or 52° *C*)	750.0	ml
Potassium dichromate (= bichromate)	12.0	gram
Sulfuric acid (concentrated)	15.0	ml
Water to make	1.0	liter

(Note: allow solution to cool before carefully adding sulfuric acid)

Clearing Bath

Water (125° *F* or 52° *C*)	750.0	ml
Sodium sulfite	100.0	gram
Water to make	1.0	liter

Second Developer

Kodak Dektol (= D-72), GAF Vividol, Printofine, or 54-D
(all developers to be used in a 1:1 dilution)

Fixer

Use any standard or rapid fixing bath

Hypo-Clearing with Toner

Working solution of hypo-eliminator . . . . (either Kodak or Perma-Wash)	1.0	quart
Kodak Rapid Selenium Toner (one time use only)	30.0	ml

REVERSAL PROCESSING STEPS

All temperatures should be 70° F (= 21° C) Use Standard Agitation throughout.

Step	Process	Time
1.	First developer	7 min., 10 sec.
2.	Water rinse (constant running water)	2 min.
3.	Bleach	3 min.
4.	Clearing	2 min.
5.	Water rinse (constant running water)	30 sec.
†6.	Wetting agent	30 sec.

Lights can be turned on at this point for rest of processing.

7. Re-exposure: hold film 12 to 14 inches from 100-watt lamp for 30 seconds each side. **Be sure no water drops are on film surface—they cause uneven exposure.**

Step	Process	Time
8.	Second developer	2 min.
9.	Water rinse (constant running water)	30 sec.
10.	Fixer	Manufacturer's minimum time.
11.	Hypo-clearing with toner (single use)	maximum of 1-1½ min.
12.	Wash	5 min.
13.	Wetting agent	30 sec.
14.	Dry and mount	

† As an alternative to steps 6 and 7, film may be developed directly after the rinse (step 5) in Kodak FD-70. This is a "fogging" developer that reduces silver halides without exposure.

Part A.	Sodium dithionite (Kodak Professional Organic Chemicals No. P533)	5.0 grams
Part B.	Water	900 ml
	Kodak Balanced Alkali	10.0 grams
	2-Thiobarbituric Acid (Kodak Professional Organic Chemicals No. 660)	0.5 grams
	Add water to make 1 liter.	

Add Part A to Part B and mix just before use. Develop for 8-9 minutes at 70° F.

REVERSAL PROCESSING OF OTHER FILMS

Recent changes in the emulsions of almost all the standard films have permitted reversal processing with a minimum of modifications of developing solutions. The complex Arneleon chemistry offered in earlier editions of the Handbook has been deleted from this edition.

Most contemporary films will respond to reversal processing when treated the same way that the "direct positive" emulsions are processed. Ocassionally the higher speed, double-coated emulsions will exhibit some signs of incomplete reversal or of residual silver that has not been removed at any point in the processing cycle. A test roll should be run of any new emulsion.

If there are patches of unchanged silver in the finished diapositive (which appear as grey densities in the highlight areas, resembling "solarizations") then the developer must first be modified by adding Sodium Thiosulfate to remove part of the silver during the first development.

Too much Thiosulfate in the first developer will cause the diapositive to appear "thin" and have a grey, rather than black, maximum density in the unexposed film surrounding the image.

If the density range of the slide is not adequate (i.e. the highlights are correctly exposed, but the shadow areas are thin) the contrast ofthe film may be increased by adding either a concentrated Hydroquinone stock, or a Sodium Hydroxide stock, or both. Since the image color is formed by the development of the residual silver (not by the development of the negative image, the additional Hydroquinone will not cause large changes in the color of the slide.

STOCK SOLUTIONS AND THEIR USE

Stock	Chemical	Quantity
1	Sodium Thiosulfate	100 grams in 1 liter of water.
2	Hydroquinone	100 grams in 500 ml of warm water. Add 100 grams of Sodium Sulfite as a preservative. Add water to make 1 liter.
3.	Sodium Hydroxide	50 grams in 500 ml cold water. After it dissolves add cold water to make 1 liter.

By using these stock solutions the following reversal processing problems can be solved:

REVERSAL PROBLEM	SOLUTION
Contrast low	Add 25-150 ml of 3 to each liter of first developer.
Max density low	Add 20-100 ml of 2 & 3 to each liter of first developer.
Partial reversal	Add 5-20 ml of 1 to each liter of first developer.

After the first development is completed, the processing steps are the same as those noted for Reversal Processing for Copying Prints. The first developer in all cases is the modified D-19.

ORTHO ROLL FILM

Very high contrast or "ortho" type film is available in 35-mm as well as in sheet film. The roll film has many uses for contemporary photocopying and printmaking. Projection slides of line copy or tables of information may be presented in correct black and white relationships but this means that the lines are black on white areas and when seen on a brightly illuminated screen the image is fatiquing and often unclear. Presenting white lines on a black screen often makes the image easy to read in brightly lighted rooms as well as in correctly darkened auditoriums.

For the printmaker the film offers advantages in that halftone images can be correctly copied directly from ink reproductions and halftone dots reused. A carefully corrected lens is needed. The Nikon MicroNikkor is probably the best lens available. It compensates automatically , making the diaphragm corrections needed as the image-to-object ratio increases (see the *Basic Photo Series*, Vol. 1, "Camera and Lens", for a discussion of bellows extension and the effect on exposure and apparent *f*-number of a lens).

Use a Micro-Nikkor, or a conventional lens with bellows or extension tubes, light the copy with two 150-watt photoflood lamps. The distance from the lamp to the center of the copyboard should be about 18 inches for material smaller than 8×10 inches. Larger originals will require greater lamp distances to avoid uneven lighting.

Expose for 1 second at *f*-8, when using KODALITH Ortho film, type 3. Develop in Kodalith Super Developer at 70° *F*, with standard agitation, for 3 minutes.

Changes in exposure and development cause large changes in the densities. Fine detail may be lost by slight increases in exposure and development. Some trial-and-error investigation will reveal the minimum exposure-development times for true blacks while retaining fine details .

Fix the film for 1½ minutes in a Rapid Fixer. For slides which have only immediate usefulness a short wash of a minute is sufficient; the thin emulsion and low-absorption base on the film permit very rapid drying. For slides that must have a long life, process carefully and dry without heat.

The ortho films are also excellent reversal materials, and may be processed by the Arneleon chemistry outlined in the *Handbook*. Small changes in chemistry, exposure and times produce large changes in density. Both continuous tone and high-contrast reversal images can be made with the ortho films.

melted gelatin for a collotype plate emulsion is filtered through a Buchner funnel; suction is supplied by an aspirator

4: non·silver prints

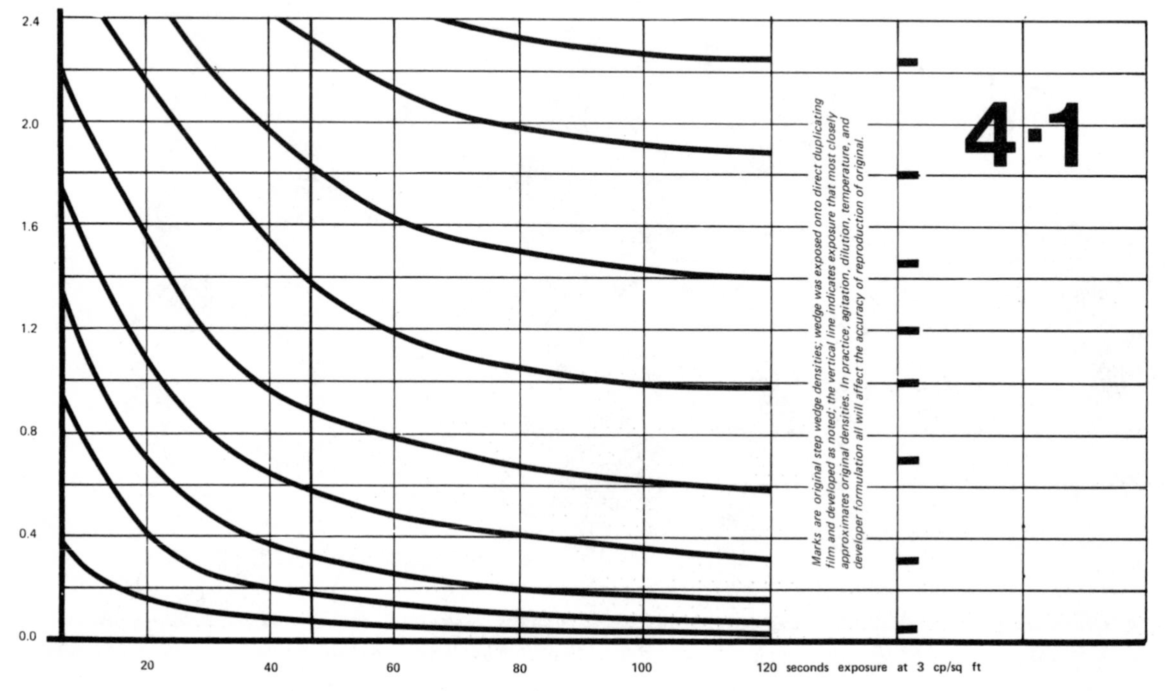

PROFESSIONAL DIRECT DUPLICATING FILM (SO-015), developed in D-72 diluted 1:3 for 2½ minutes at 70° F, in tray, continuous agitation.

The silver print is the major print process surviving the experimentation of the nineteenth century. Other print processes are available: electrical, thermal, and dye-destruction. Some commercially obsolete processes have contemporary value.

These processes require a contact negative or positive. Gum and platinum need negatives. Gravure requires a continuous tone positive. Silkscreen requires a halftone positive. Obtaining any of the intermediate masters requires careful manipulation of film and chemicals.

Iron salts are moderately photosensitive. They can be combined with other metals, as in the platinum and palladium process, or can be used directly as in the ferrocyanotype. All the iron salt processes are slow. They require long exposure to bright light. A mercury vapor lamp or a bank of UV fluorescent tubes is convenient.

Other materials are photosensitive in that they change hardness or solubility when exposed to light. Gum process prints use the change of solubility of chromated gum arabic when exposed to light. Silkscreen and gravure resists depend on the fact that the melting point of gelatin, sensitized with a chromate, is higher after exposure to light.

ENLARGED NEGATIVES

The best negative for any print is always an original. This requires a viewcamera for a large format negative and the subject itself often prohibits the use of the large camera.

An enlarged negative may be an enlarged film positive printed onto another piece of film, producing a copy negative. There is always distortion of the tonal scale, though this can be minimized by careful placement of the exposure when making the intermediate positive.

The intermediate film positive should not have hard blacks and clear highlights. To have either will place the image near the shoulder or the toe of the characteristic curve of the positive film material. This distorts the tones when the image is printed to make the final negative.

GAF Versapan and KODAK Super XX are suitable films.

A second way to make enlarged negatives is by reversal processing. Any black and white film can be processed to produce direct copy. The Arneleon chemistry permits controlled reversal processing. A negative can be enlarged directly to a negative.

A third way to produce enlarged duplicate negatives is by using the KODAK Professional Direct Duplicating Film (SO-015). This film has been manufactured so that it is "exposed" to the top of the d-log-e curve. Any additional exposure will cause *decreasing* density.

The film is made for duplicating continuous tone negatives and is a recent addition to the Kodak catalogue, and in fact the emulsion number is a temporary one which will be replaced when additional marketing research indicates a final form is ready for sale. It is similar to the High Speed Duplicating Film used for line copy work in that it is orthochromatic, though lower in contrast.

A parametric presentation of the characteristics of the film is shown in Figure 4-1. This parametric differs from those in Section 3 because the film has been exposed to a calibrated step-wedge, and developed for a constant time. The variable here is the exposure time of the entire set of information points. The development time was determined by making a preliminary set of parametrics in which development times for a trial exposure were tried, attempting to produce a set of curves with separations similar to the original step-wedge densities.

The film is relatively insensitive, with a trial exposure time of 40 seconds with an enlarger set to produce an 8 X 10 inch patch at an f-5.6 aperture (typical for most contemporary enlargers except the Omega B-22, which would require an f-8 lens setting). Insufficient exposure will cause the shadow areas of the copy negative to be crushed (as these are still on the "shoulder" of the copy film), and the highlight densities to be exaggerated, and yet still dense. Overexposure will cause exaggerated separations of the shadow tones and loss of detail in the highlights, as these areas would be overexposed and "run off the curve."

The film shows normal sensitivity to overall density/development controls. The overall density shift of the maximum density available rises from about 1.5 at 1½ minutes development in D-72 diluted 1:3 and used at 70 degrees F to almost 3.0 when development is continued for 6 minutes.

INTERMEDIATE POSITIVES

For gravure, silkscreen and for making a negative print by any print process an intermediate positive is required. This may be either continuous tone or a high-contrast image. The positive can be made on film or paper.

Continuous tone positives are easily made by printing a negative onto KODAK Fine Grain Positive film. This film has an emulsion that can be handled under ordinary darkroom safelights. It is sensitive to exposure-development controls. Increasing development time increases contrast. About three number grades of contrast control are attainable with development time changes.

More contrasty positives can be made from films made for lithography. When processed as recommended these "line" emulsions produce either black or clear emulsion. If developed in dilute paper developer they make a continuous tone positive. Each film has a different character. GAF Reproline film works well. Develop it in D-72 for 40" to 1½ minutes.

Paper prints themselves can be used as intermediate positives for several of the print processes. The paper base has too much density for use with any of the non-silver processes but it can be used to expose litho films for making a high contrast intermediate negative. A paper positive can be used to expose paper prints. Wet both of them with water and squeegee them together, emulsion to emulsion. An enlarger can be used as a light source to expose the new print through the paper base of the positive. Because the image is in the emulsion, next to the new print, the texture of the paper support has little effect.

HALFTONE CONVERSIONS

For silkscreen (and zinc intaglio) change the continuous grey tones of the photographic image into spots or lines separated by white. If these units are small enough they will be averaged by the eye into grey.

There are a number of ways to change continuous tone images to halftone equivalents. One is to copy the image (using a process camera) through a glass halftone ruled screen which is, in its effect, a field of tiny lenses that change the copy subject into dots of varying size. Grey tones are converted into tiny spots of emulsion. These cannot be separated by the ey. If the dots are large and close together the effect is of dark grey. If small and separate, of light grey.

This also can be done by using KODAK Autoscreen. This film is a high contrast emulsion pre-exposed to a halftone screen. The latent image of the screen adds to the image creating a fine halftone dot pattern. The screen pattern contains 133 lines of dots in each inch.

A coarse halftone image that can be reproduced by silkscreen can be made by projecting the Autoscreen film with an enlarger. A usable coarse dot pattern results.

A second way to create a halftone conversion is by a "tone-line" conversion (see Figure 4-1). This converts the grey image into lines speckles or blank areas. The more texture in the original, the more detail there will be in the conversion. Untextured areas of the original appear white or black.

The original negative or an enlarged negative may be used in a tone-line conversion. In either case the negative is contact printed onto either Fine Grain Positive or Reproline film (0.055 base). The positive produced should look dark and of normal contrast. When examined against the bottom of a white darkroom tray it will look like an overexposed print of normal contrast. The whites will appear grey; some of the shadows will seem too dark. Viewed as a transparency there will be full shadow detail.

Dry the film print. Tape the negative emulsion down to the glass of a contact printing frame. 3M's Magic Transparent Tape No. 810 is good. It is thin and the adhesive does not bleed. Place the film print over the negative, emulsion up. Bring them into exact register, and tape them. The images are assembled into a sandwich, in register but with the emulsions separated.

The assembly, viewed with transmitted light, appears nearly balanced but the positive image is stronger than the negative. The sensation is that of looking at a very dull and flat print.

In the darkroom place a piece of litho film on top of the positive-negative sandwich and close the printing frame. Hold the frame under the enlarger at about a 45 degree angle. With the enlarger set for 11 X 14 inch prints, the lens set at *f*-8, and the timer at 10 seconds, expose the slanted printing frame. Turn the frame a quarter turn, maintain the same angle, and expose again. Repeat this for all sides.

Light passes through the slots left between positive and negative images in register but separated by two thicknesses of film base. Properly exposed and developed the film will blacken where the image was exposed between the positive and negative emulsions and remain clear elsewhere.

Develop the film in a two-part developer designed for litho negatives. Developing time at 75° *F* will be 3 to 5 minutes. If the image appears before two minutes the film is overexposed or the sandwich is too thin.

A third way to make conversions is to enlarge a continuous tone negative onto litho film. A paper developer is used (D-72, 1:15). This will produce a granular contrasty image. Careful exposure and development will permit high, medium, or low values to be retained. Splice positives together to produce a composite positive. The images for light, medium, or dark tonal areas may be printed sequentially (by silkscreen or gum process); a "posterization" effect is achieved.

With halftone processes the print process itself controls the esthetics. Trying to emulate the silver print with another process will usually misfire.

Non-silver processes can be of use to the photographer, the printmaker, and artist who wishes to incorporate continuous tone images into prints or paintings.

A "random" screen can be generated by using textured "non-glare" glass used for framing prints. A slightly different texture exists on each side of the glass, and when the glass is laid with the coarser texture next to the emulsion of a litho film and an image projected onto the film through the glass, the image will be broken into tiny random patterns of black and clear emulsion. as a function of the high contrast character of the film.

Contrast can be controlled experimentally by determining the correct exposure for the shadow details in the positive halftone that results from the projection of a negative on lithographic film, and then removing the glass screen from over the film and exposing to "flash" exposure of 30-60 seconds. The second exposure is provided by an OA safelight about 3 feet from the film. This second exposure adds density to the highlights without appreciably affecting the shadows, and reduces the overall density range (as transformed to dot sizes).

DENSITOMETER CONTROL OF PRINT EXPOSURE

Silver printing lends itself to trial-and-error methods that are both expensive and wasteful. Because one can quickly see the results of a trial exposure, little thought is given to making two or three trial prints. Platinum, palladium, gum, gravure and other processes prohibit this because of material cost and because of delays between the test exposures and the validation in the print.

Step. 1. Examine the negative. It may be well to make a silver print for study purposes. Determine the Zone VIII areas. Choose one that is large enough to be meterable with the densitometer. Determine the density of this area. For a normal negative it will be about 1.30 (somewhere between 1.15 and 1.45). Verify that the shadow densities are normal (about 0.30 for first important shadow areas).

Step 2. Make a good print with platinum. This means trial-and-error until you learn what a good print looks like and how the materials should be handled. Keep a notebook record. When you have a good print, note the exact conditions. This is now a standard print. The negative that made it is a standard negative.

Step 3. To print a new negative, first measure its Zone VIII density. Then proceed down a series of steps as outlined below;

3a. New density 1.20

3b. Standard density 1.30 (for example)

3c. (subtract line 3b from 3a to obtain the difference)

Difference −0.10

A correction must be made from the O/T table below. Note the algebraic sign of the difference. Since it is negative, refer to the T column opposite a density of 0.10 in the O/T table. T = 0.79. If it had been positive, the O column of the table would be used.

3d. Correction factor X 0.79

3e. Standard exposure 15.0 minutes (from trial-and-error)

3f. New exposure (line 3d X 3e) 11.8 minutes

This will produce a correct highlight density exposure from the new negative. In tabular form the computation is:

1.	New density	D_n
2.	Standard density	D_s
3.	Difference	$D_s - D_n$ (− = T; + = O)
4.	Correction	(from O/T table)
5.	Standard exposure	Minutes
6.	New exposure (4X5)	Minutes

A SHORT TABLE OF OPACITY (O) AND TRANSMISSION (T) FOR PRINTING EXPOSURES

Density	O	T	Density	O	T	Density	O	T
0.00	1.00	1.00	0.10	1.26	0.79	0.20	1.58	0.63
0.01	1.02	0.98	0.11	1.29	0.78	0.21	1.62	0.66
0.02	1.05	0.96	0.12	1.32	0.76	0.22	1.66	0.60
0.03	1.07	0.93	0.13	1.35	0.74	0.23	1.70	0.59
0.04	1.10	0.91	0.14	1.38	0.72	0.24	1.75	0.57
0.05	1.12	0.89	0.15	1.41	0.71	0.25	1.78	0.56
0.06	1.15	0.87	0.16	1.44	0.70	0.26	1.82	0.55
0.07	1.18	0.74	0.17	1.48	0.68	0.27	1.86	0.54
0.08	1.20	0.83	0.18	1.51	0.66	0.28	1.90	0.52
0.09	1.23	0.81	0.19	1.55	0.65	0.29	1.95	0.51
						0.30	1.99	0.50

A table of 0.00 to 3.00 is published in the Photo Lab Index, p. 16 - 140.

THE PLATINUM PRINT

Certain iron salts are photosensitive. By contemporary standards they are not "fast". All require long exposure. Of itself iron is not a dependable base for an image, it oxidizes easily.

This can be overcome by linking the iron to a more stable metal, eliminating the iron after the image is fixed. The platinum process links platinum (an inert metal) and iron. After development the iron is etched away. Only inert platinum is left.

The emulsion must be compounded by the photographer who paints it on the print paper. Platinum images can be printed on paper before printing gum gravure or lithograph.

The process requires a contact negative. Development is in a simple solution, clearing in an acid solution, and a short wash.

PREPARING PAPER FOR PLATINUM PRINTING

The print is only as permanent as the support. The more sulfur in the paper, the shorter the print's life. The paper also affects the image--the smoothness of the tonal scale. Platinum-iron salts react unpredictably with trace elements of minerals. Some cheap papers produce better images than good papers!

A good paper to use is RIVES BFK. It is lightly textured, with a warm white color. Size it before using. Sizing closes pores of the paper, preventing the salts from penetrating deeply. Size assists the adhesion of the salts and makes possible their even distribution.

Sizing affects image color, tonal scale, and brilliance. Traditional sizes are starch, gelatin, and arrowroot. Experience with gelatin has been disappointing. Emulsion sensitivity is poor and contrast is flat. Starch sizing has been most satisfactory. For intermedia work this is a good size. It causes little physical change in the surface of the paper that could interfere with subsequent printing.

Cooked starch penetrates and provides a permanent base. Place a tablespoon of ARGO white starch in a pyrex or new enamelware saucepan. Use a wooden or plastic spoon. Add enough cold water to dissolve the starch. Make a thin paste. Heat two cups of water to boiling and add it to the paste, stirring constantly. Heat this mixture until it boils for three to five minutes. Use it warm: it will gel on cooling. Spread it evenly with a small sponge. Allow the paper to dry. Resize to insure complete sealing. Store the paper flat.

THE NEGATIVE FOR PLATINUM PRINTING

Platinum has a straight line response. It does not crush shadow details. Whatever is on the negative will appear on the print. Shadows should be rendered with great clarity. The negative should be normal. Best prints are light density about 1.30 to 1.40. Even small negatives make good contact prints. Color of the image, sensation of depth, and the tactile qualities of the print are all different with the platinum print compared with the silver print. Aaron Scharf once remarked the esthetic problem of the photograph is that the image "floats"-- is not attached to the surface of the paper. The platinum image has a physical presence unmatched in photographic prints. Certain subjects respond to printing with platinum salts to produce prints of special beauty. The image color and tactility will not be appropriate to all images.

If a 35-mm camera is used, an enlarged negative can be made by one of the processes outlined earlier in the *Handbook.*

PLATINUM PROCESS CHEMICALS

The quantities of the chemicals listed will permit an exploration of the process. Many of the chemicals are hard to obtain from local sources; check chemical suppliers in major cities.

The price of platinum salts is rising steadily, and may well be beyond the budget of all but the most dedicated experimenter.

The Photosensitive Emulsion:

Oxalic Acid	100 grams
Ferric Oxalate	100 grams
Potassium Chlorate	100 grams
Potassium Chloroplatinite	2 grams

The Platinum Process Developer:

Potassium Oxalate	500 grams

The Clearing Bath:

Hydrochloric Acid	1 liter

MIXING AND USING PLATINUM EMULSIONS

The emulsion is mixed from three stable stock solutions. These are combined just before spreading onto the sized paper. They may be stored in medicine dropper bottles. Because of the cost of the platinum salts, only mix emulsion to coat one 8×10 inch sheet at a time.

SOLUTION A

Water, hot	60.0 ml
Oxalic acid	1.1 grams
Ferric oxalate	16.0 grams

SOLUTION B

Water, hot	60.0 ml
Oxalic acid	1.1 grams
Ferric oxalate	16.0 grams
Potassium chlorate	0.3 grams

SOLUTION C

Water	60.0 ml
Potassium chloroplatinite	12.0 grams

This is a large amount of platinum. A smaller quantity may be used in a proportionately smaller volume of water. For example, 3 grams of platinum may be dissolved in 14 ml of water.

The platinum salt will dissolve slowly. Solutions A and B are rusty in color. Solution C is a deep red-brown.

The sensitivity of the emulsion is very low. It may be mixed in dim room light (avoiding direct exposure from fluorescent or window lights) and dried in a dark room. It dries quickly. Ten minutes is sufficient. The moisture must be driven out by heat to insure clear highlights. Lay it on an electric hotplate for a few seconds; move it smoothly and rapidly to that no part of the paper is overheated and scorched. Use it immediately.

The emulsion is easily spread with a flat Japanese brush. This brush is sewn to a wooden handle. It contains no metal that could contaminate the emulsion. A brush about 1½ inches wide can be obtained for $2.00 from Aiko's Art Materials Import, 714 North Wabash Avenue, Chicago, Illinois 60611. The round brushes absorb too much of the platinum. One layer of bristles on the flat brush can be trimmed off, reducing the loss of platinum but not reducing the spreading ability of the brush. Wet the brush with water before using, then squeeze it out.

A small quantity of the emulsion is mixed and spread on the paper. Prepare paper for printing by first outlining the area to be printed. Pour out a line of emulsion along one edge of the printing area; rapidly paint this across the paper toward the opposite edge. Pour the rest of the emulsion along the opposite edge and paint back toward the starting place. The quantity of emulsion suggested in the mixing instructions will luxuriantly cover an 8×10 inch area (or five 4×5 inch prints). Always work on clean surfaces. Any trace of iron causes stains.

PLATINUM EMULSION CONTRAST MIXTURES

CONTRASTY NEGATIVES (with normal shadow density and highlight densities about 1.50)

Solution A	22 drops
Solution B	0 drops
Solution C	24 drops

NORMAL NEGATIVES (with highlight densities about 1.30)

Solution A	14 drops
Solution B	8 drops
Solution C	24 drops

FLAT NEGATIVES (with highlight densities about 1.10)

Solution A	8 drops
Solution B	14 drops
Solution C	24 drops

Measuring "by the drop" is accurate enough and repeatable in practice. The dropper cap is squeezed until a drop falls free by its own weight. A fourth dropper bottle is convenient for containing the combined solutions.

The same amount of platinum is used in all emulsions. The amount of Potassium Chlorate controls contrast. The higher the contrast, the more granular the image. Also, with higher contrast emulsions it is likely that brushing patterns will show. This may or may not be a problem, depending on the uses of the image. Shake the emulsion to combine the stocks and pour it out. The sizing will prevent immediate penetration. There will be 10 to 15 seconds in which to manipulate the emulsion before it sinks into the paper. Paint all areas where image is desired. The dried emulsion is a pale ochre.

PLATINUM PRINTING

The print should be exposed as soon as the emulsion is dry. Sunlight may be used but it is irregular in intensity. The emulsion is insensitive to yellow or red light. A sunlamp or UV lamp is best. A mercury vapor lamp or a battery of six 12-inch UV fluorescents are good sources of light. At 15 inches the exposure for a mercury vapor lamp is about 20 minutes.

The emulsion shows some printing-out of the image. If the contact print frame is half-opened and the paper lifted away from the negative a pale lavender image can be seen. This image is not a dependable indicator of correct exposure. Experimental exposures using time and lamp-to-frame distance variations will provide exposure guides.

The three emulsion mixtures have different printing speeds. The low contrast (A) emulsion is faster than the others. It requires about 25% less exposure than B. The high contrast (C) emulsion is quite slow and requires at least 60% more exposure than B for similar highlight densities. Densitometer readings of highlight densities can be correlated to exposure times for a given contrast emulsion.

A traditional way to minimize waste is to coat an oversize piece of paper with an emulsion, then trim out an area the size of the negative. The trimmings with the smears of emulsion are used as test strips. Expose and develop strips to determine exposure times for a negative.

DEVELOPING THE PLATINUM PRINT

The developer is a solution of Potassium Oxalate. Dissolve one pound in 48 ounces of water. This solution will gradually be used up; about one ounce of developer is carried off with each 8×10 inch piece of RIVES BFK paper.

The developer may be used over a wide temperature range. At higher temperatures it is necessary to immerse the print with a single smooth gesture. A line will appear if the immersion stops at any point.

At low temperatures (65° *F*) full development may take a minute. At high temperatures (110° *F*) development is immediate. Allow the print to stay in the solution twice the apparent development time. There is no continuing development. A print cannot be "saved" in development.

The print "dries down" sharply. Highlights should be printed for the least visible detail. When dry they will appear in Zone VII.

CLEARING AND WASHING THE PRINT

After development the image contains both platinum and iron. For permanence, the iron must be removed. It is taken out by a weak Hydrochloric Acid solution. The Clearing Solution is made by mixing 2/3 ounce of hydrochloric acid with one quart of water. Use at 70 to 90° *F*.

Clear in three sequential acid baths. Separate stocks should be used. The print is placed in the first bath, agitated normally and after 3 to 4 minutes moved to the second bath. The process is repeated for the second and third baths. The third bath must be water clear when the process is finished or there is still iron left in the print. At the end of washing, the third bath is moved up one step, the second becomes the first, and the first is dumped. This way there is always fresh acid for the last rinse.

Wash the print in a print-washing tray for 10 minutes to remove the acid. Dry the print. It may be waxed for greater clarity of shadow detail. Use a hard paste wax. The print may be dry mounted or over-matted. Ordinary spotting colors, or an HB lead pencil, may be used for spotting. The finished image is brown-black. More neutral grey-black images were produced with the chemistry available when the process was in general use; contemporary support paper generally create a warmer image. Coating with a more dilute emulsion (1:1 with distilled water) and sensitizing twice also provides a more neutral image.

PALLADIUM PRINT CHEMISTRY

The working chemistry of palladium is nearly identical to that of platinum. The handling of the emulsion is the same. The C solution of the emulsion is compounded as follows:

Water	60 ml
Sodium Chloropalladate	9 grams

A smaller quantity may be mixed.

OTHER CONTRAST CONTROLS

Increasing exposure time will increase contrast. This is done by increasing lamp-print distance. For platinum only (not palladium) potassium bichromate may be added to the developer 1 gram per liter); this is equivalent to ½ paper grade in silver print notation.

THE CYANOTYPE

This makes a blue image on a white background. The photographs by Gustav LeSecq and some of the prints by Clarence White (in the Museum of Modern Art Collection) were done using similar iron salts.

The paper may be sized with strach, or an egg albumin may be used to harden the surface. This sizing is made by beating the whites of four large eggs. Discard the yolks. Let the whites sit overnight after beating. Float the paper in a mixture of whites and distilled water. Use 4 parts egg white, one part water. This thins the albumen enough to make it easier to work with. Size the paper for one minute and then hang it to dry.

Mix the emulsion as shown:

EMULSION STOCK SOLUTIONS

A.	Ammonio-citrate of iron	50 gram
	Water	250 ml
B.	Potassium ferricyanide	35 gram
	Water	250 ml

(Use distilled or deionized water. Store solutions in dark bottles or in the darkroom)

To use mix equal volumes of A and B. Place in a flat plastic or glass tray. Float the sized paper on the solution. Hold it by opposite corners and let the middle sag onto the solution. Let the ends slip down without capturing bubbles underneath. Sensitize for three minutes, then hang to dry in the dark. Print as soon as the paper is dry. Contact print by inspection. Exposures run about 30 minutes with a mercury vapor lamp at 15 inches. The image appears reddish-bronze; the unexposed paper is yellow-green. Wash the print in clear water until all remaining yellow is cleared. A few drops of hydrochloric acid will intensify the blue if added to the first wash. Useful results can be had be sensitizing colored papers.

BICHROMATE-BASED IMAGES

Many natural gums and colloids may be made photosensitive with a bichromate solution. Light will either harden the colloid or change the solubility of the gum. The change is proportional to exposure.

There are two effects of the bichromate that do not occur with other photosensitive materials. One is that once sensitized the material will immediately begin to change state, becoming more and more insoluble or hardened. At first this appears to be an increase in printing sensitivity or "speed". But if not used within a few days the emulsion will be self-hardened, without the action of light.

The second effect is called "continuing action". A certain exposure will cause a given change of physical state; unless the bichromate is immediately washed out the exposure will produce a continuing change in the emulsion. Because of the exposure it will continue to change, becoming more hardened or more insoluble.

Bichromated emulsions should be used as soon as they are dry after being sensitized. They should be processed immediately after exposure to obtain repeatable results. The bichromate usually used for photosensitizing is Potassium Bichromate because it is cheaper than other bichromate salts. Ammonium Dichromate is perceptibly "faster" however. Note that Dichromate and Bichromate are synonomous terms.

CAUTION: **exposure to chromates sensitizes skin and produces "chromic acid poisoning." Always wear rubber gloves when sensitizing gelatin gravure tissues, or when handling chromate sensitizers for gum solutions.**

THE GUM PRINT

The gum (or gum-bichromate) print is made by placing an emulsion of watercolor and bichromated gum arabic onto sized paper. After drying, the emulsion is exposed by contact with a UV light source. The image is developed by floating the print on water. The water penetrates the gum and permits the unhardened gum to dissolve. Development takes 30 minutes. After one layer has dried, the paper may be coated with new gum and exposed again. Different colors may be used in whole or in part for each emulsion layer.

The effect of the gum print is variable. An approximation of the silver print is possible. But the process is naturally adaptable to a manipulated image where color, texture, and other manipulations are desired.

The literature available on the gum print is extensive. The following is a working outline of the procedure.

PREPARATION FOR PRINTING

Size the paper and prepare the gum. Each process takes several days.

Powdered gum arabic is available from all professional chemical supply houses. To a liter of water add 300 to 350 grams of gum arabic. Mix by shaking and then allow to stand for three days to dissolve completely. Distilled water should be used. To prevent bacterial growth, add 2.5 grams of Mercuric Chloride as a preservative. **Mercuric chloride is a deadly poison.** After dissolving, the gum solution has a light tan color and is of syrupy consistency.

The paper may be smooth or textured. A lightly textured paper (Rives BFK) is suitable for many images. The paper must be sized. Gum often requires several layers of emulsion, so sizing must be thorough. The sturdiest sizing is gelatin, hardened with formalin. Apply it in two layers: the second fills tiny bubbles left in the first.

For dimensional stability the paper must be presoaked. Rives paper, for example, will swell and increase its length about 15% the first time it is wetted. Soak the paper for gum printing in hot water (100° *F*) for ten minutes before sizing.

Knox or A & P gelatin is satisfactory. Some other chain store proprietary brands tend to clump. Three packets of gelatin are poured into one quart of cold water (50 to 60° *F*). It will swell, absorbing most of the water. After 15 minutes warm it to 100° *F*. Two or three quarts of size are necessary for an even coating. Immerse the sheet of paper in the size. Draw the paper out under a glass rod (about 3/8 or 1/2 inch in diameter—the rods provided for towel racks are suitable). The rod will break down bubbles and smooth out irregular places. Hang the sheets to dry on a line strung with clothes pins.

When the first layer is dry repeat the sizing. After two layers have been applied, harden them by floating the sheets on a solution of formalin. The hardener is formaldehyde 37%, available at most drugstores. Use 25 ml in a liter of water. Use the hardener in a well ventilated room.

Certain of the spray starches seem to provide acceptable sealing for single-printing. Insufficient sizing will produce general color staining. The pigment used to produce the image will cling to the fibers of the paper, causing color fog.

A soft negative will work best if the result desired is an emulation of the silver print. Line negatives, and other high contrast negatives, work well for vigorous prints and produce color statements with tactile richness.

GUM SENSITIZING

Potassium or Ammonium Dichromate may be used to sensitize the gum. Ammonium is faster in printing speed.

Use a saturated solution. The sensitizer is then added to the gum in small quantities, not diluting the gum excessively.

GUM SENSITIZER

Ammonium (or Potassium) Dichromate	29 grams
Water, hot	75 ml

(dissolve, then add cold water to make 100 ml)

Below 70° *F* some of the salt will precipitate out. Warm it before using. Equal quantities of saturated sensitizer and gum mixed with pigment are used. Disposable one-ounce medical plastic cups are suggested for measuring gum solutions. The gum's viscosity gives it a large meniscus. The one-ounce cups are well marked and large enough in diameter to minimize the effect of the meniscus.

Once mixed the gum begins to become insoluble. After several days it is useless. For accurate printing it is best to coat the mixture immediately after combining and to use the paper as soon as the gum emulsion dries.

Coat the emulsion with a brush. It may be fiber or a polyfoam plastic spreader. Brushing the gum aerates it and causes it to set. Work quickly; then dry the paper in the dark. Contrary to statements published in older texts, bichromate emulsions are photosensitive when wet. Work in dim room light, away from fluorescents and window light.

Older texts call for a blending brush. This is necessary only for simulating the silver print.

PIGMENTS FOR THE GUM PROCESS

WINDSOR AND NEWTON watercolors and the GRUMBACHER gouache colors are dependable and provide definite colors with the least amount of flaking. Other watercolors do not have enough pigment density. PRANG poster colors produce broad effects (see Section 5: Color Prints, for details on three-color gum printing).

Notes should be kept on amounts of pigment and gum used for a print. Pigment to gum ratios that have been successful with contemporary materials are 5 to 10 grams of pigment in 100 ml of gum (before sensitizer is added). The gouaches provide excellent solid-color area statements. The watercolor pigments provide good continuous tone images. High contrast negatives used with gouach produce images similar to silkscreen statements but with more luminosity. SHIVA waterbase block printing inks also work well for strong color.

EXPOSING THE DEVELOPING THE GUM PRINT

The bichromate sensitized gum is hardened only by blue and ultraviolet light. A mercury lamp is best. With a standard sun lamp at 20 inches an exposure of 3 to 6 minutes is sufficient. A two-tube desk model fluorescent lamp will expose small prints satisfactorily. Exposure is about 25 minutes at 12 inches. Overexposure can be reduced by extended development; underexposure cannot be helped by shortened development.

Develop in plain water, immediately after exposing. This prevents image changes caused by "continuing action", i.e., hardening begun by light that will continue even when the light is removed. Several trays of water at 80° *F* work best. The print is immersed by sliding the paper in smoothly, emulsion up. After 40 to 60 seconds the paper will be wetted. Lift it by one end and then lay it face down onto the water. It will float.

Rocking the tray causes irregular development. Development is water penetrating the gum and dissolving the unhardened gum next to the paper. This disperses into the water. Eventually the hardened gum adheres to the paper; this is the image.

Development may be speeded by sliding the paper carefully out of the water and reinserting it. This reduces the development time to about 15 minutes. With still water total development takes about one hour. The paper should be moved from one tray to fresh water in the next tray every quarter-hour to prevent pigment redepositing itself onto the print. Lampblack is most prone to staining.

Development is finished when the yellow chromate stain disappears from the back of the paper. Gum prints can be combined with other prints and with drawings. After printing a platinum, paint-on-silver emulsion, lithographic or intaglio image, size the paper, sensitize, and print. The inks will not be reduced by the additional wetting

PHOTOGRAVURE

All ink processes (excepting the Woodbury type) are "halftone" processes; the ink has only one color, yet can appear to be any tone of grey if it is applied to the paper in spots of varying sizes, separated by white areas of about the same size. When the spots and separations are small the eye cannot resolve them and they average into grey.

There are two ways of creating spots fo controlled size. One is to impose a mechanical grid over the image. This is done with glass screens, magenta contact screens, Autoscreen film, and with texture screens. Lithographic and relief printing use dots of varying size. Gravure uses dots of varying depth.

Photogravure uses ink to make the image; it is a photomechanical process. Light is used to harden a sheet of gelatin. The hardened sheet is adhered to a sheet of copper. The gelatin-copper sandwich is immersed in an etchant that is controlled by the resin. When the etching is complete the gelatin resist is removed, the holes in the copper are inked, and a print is made. Several hundred prints can be made from a copper plate if it is reinforced with a steel surface; at least a hundred prints can be made from an unsurfaced plate.

The gravure process requires an etching press and inking and wiping facilities. The acid etchants normally used on copper are not used in gravure; an Iron etchant is used because a Hydrogen etchant cannot be controlled by a gelatin photoresist.

The primary etching control is the resist. This is a sheet of gelatin sensitized with bichromate. When exposed to light the sensitized gelatin changes; its melting point rises, proportional to the amount of exposure.

The resist is exposed through a positive. This is adhered to a copper plate. The plate has been prepared by being dusted with a fine coating of rosin or asphaltum powder. The resist is then developed by washing away the unhardened gelatin in hot water. After developing, the gelatin is dried. The image is etched with an iron compound (not acid). The large iron molecule migrates slowly through the gelatin. It permits differential etching; fast where the resist is thin, slow where it is thick.

After etching, the resist is washed away with water; the aquatint powder melted on the surface is dissolved and scrubbed off. The plate is warmed; ink rubbed into the etched holes. When these holes are full, the surface of the copper is wiped clean. The plate is put onto an etching press. Paper that has been soaked to soften the fibers is placed on the plate. Several felt pads are placed over that and the entire assembly is passed through heavy rollers. The ink is lifted out of the holes on the plate, captured by the fibers of the paper. When the paper is peeled away, the image is presented in ink rather than silver or platinum. The appearance is of a continuous tone image. Only close inspection reveals the halftone image.

Handwiped (or sheet-fed) gravure differs from rotogravure in that the screen pattern is random. The eye does not sense the imposition of a screen structure on the image.

THE POSITIVE

A film positive is used to expose the resist. The minimum density should be about 0.50 in the important highlight areas. The darkest shadow areas should be about 1.30. The positive seen lying wet on the bottom of a plastic tray looks like a conventional print that has been overexposed almost a full stop.

The positive used with rosin grounds can be higher in contrast than one for asphaltum grounds. The rosin pattern is inevitably more coarse; it reduces the apparent contrast of the image. The asphaltum retains finer detail and allows deeper etching. The resist material will also affect the degree of contrast desired in a positive. The Chemco tissue will accept a more contrasty positive than the McGraw Colorgraph type 47. Begin with a positive that appears flat; etch in a denser etching bath. Do not attempt to work with a contrasty positive.

The best film for a positive is Fine Grain Positive. Use standard paper safelights. It has about the same speed as conventional paper.

To make a contact-positive, set the enlarger to illuminate an 11 × 14 inch area, with a 4 × 5 inch carrier in the enlarger stage. With the lens at *f*-16, a trial exposure of 10″ and development for 1 to 1½ minutes in Dektol 1:2 at 70° *F* will yield a reasonable positive. Dry this and measure its densities. Visual examination is not sufficiently accurate for control. If the print highlight densities are less than 0.50, increase the exposure. If the shadow densities exceed 1.30, decrease the development time. Careful handling is necessary to achieve dependable and predictable results. Insert the piece of film into the developer with a smooth single stroke. Agitate constantly. Do not rock the tray—this produces greater densities near the edges compared with the middle and often produces muddy or poorly articulated tones in the center. Lift and turn the film frequently.

When the positive transparency is complete, opaque a ¼-inch band with silver 3M mylar tape or the red acetate tape sold by graphic supply houses. Both have an adhesive that will not smear with age, is thin, and is photographically opaque.

SENSITIZING THE RESIST

The resist is a sheet of animal gelatin coated on a paper support. It has a red color due to iron oxide added to assist in visually assessing development. It becomes photosensitive only after being sensitized with Bichromate. It is easily damaged—do not crack the emulsion by bending it sharply. Do not allow it to become too hot, too dry, or too damp.

The sensitizing solution is a 3.5% Potassium Bichromate solution. This is mixed at 100° *F* and then chilled to 55° *F* for use. Wear rubber gloves when working with any chromate: it will sensitize the skin and produce an allergic reaction.

At present there is only one supplier of photogravure resist materials in this country. MCGRAW-COLORGRAPH, 175 West Verdugo Boulevard, Burbank, California 91503. Their photogravure resist tissue Type 37 is most useful for sheet-fed gravure. It is described as "moderate contrast, for the single-bath etching system." Since a modification of this is what is suggested, this material works well. Type 47 is also available but seems to have a steeper response curve and is for conventional multi-bath etching. The McGraw resist is shipped flat, in precut sheets. It is more expensive but stores better and is easier to handle because it is provided in sheet form.

The resist is sensitized in safe-light or low-level tungsten light. The sensitizer is 35 grams of Bichromate in a liter of water. Chill to 55° *F*. The resist is slipped in, face up. It softens and swells quickly: damage can be done to the surface. Do not add wetting agent to the sensitizer. This is mentioned in the McGraw Gravure Handbook but it destroys the ability of the tissue to adhere by the "wet mounting" process used with flat copper plates. Soak the tissue 3 minutes.

While the tissue is soaking, prepare the drying surface. This is a piece of plexiglass without the protective paper. It should be wiped clean, and washed in cold water. A piece of opaque white scrap is suitable for test developing trial resists, as well as for drying resists after sensitizing. The plexiglass should be 1/4-inch thick—thinner plastic flexes too much.

When the tissue is well soaked, lift it by two corners and allow it to drain onto the plexiglass. The plexiglass should be on a firm, flat, clean working surface. Position the resist and place it on the plastic. With a firm gentle stroke squeegee the sensitizer off the resist. Use a Kodak blade squeegee. The resist is placed face down onto the plastic so the squeegee strokes the supporting paper. Stroke from the center out. Blot any puddles from the resist with paper towels. Set it in a cool place to dry. If a fan is used to accelerate and produce more even drying, do not point it at the resist but above it. The fan must move the air away, not blow on the resist. The resist dries in about 45 minutes and pops off the plastic. If it begins to peel back at a corner (because of uneven drying) it can be saved by covering the peeling section with a piece of heavy cardboard. Uneven drying produces wrinkles in the gelatin that will prevent the resist from making contact with the positive.

The dry resist will have an immaculate, mirror-smooth surface. It should be used at once. After sensitization it begins to harden. It will be totally useless in a few days and about 7% "faster" at the end of 24 hours.

Expose the resist by a mercury vapor lamp. A correctly made resist requires 5 to 10 minutes exposure at 20 inches. Precise distance and time must be determined by trial-and-error. Overheating may be a problem. If a "sun-lamp" is used, a large amount of heat is radiated: cool the surface of the print-frame glass with an electric fan.

ADHERING THE RESIST

The resist must be developed at once. There is a "continuing action" in bichromated materials; once the photosensitive material has been exposed, it continues to harden with time, even though the light has stopped.

The following procedure has been developed to combat the variable temperatures and humidities encountered in school working conditions. The technical literature on gravure presumes constant humidity and temperatures not possible in most non-professional environments.

Place the resist in a safe dry place. Place the prepared copper plate (its preparation will be described later) face up in a tray of warm deionized water at 80 to 85° *F*. Rest it on a wire "W". This is a support to keep the plate off the bottom of the tray. It can then be picked up easily without damaging the prepared ground.

Slip the resist into a tray of cold deionized water at 65° *F*. Put it in face up to be sure it is wetted evenly. Lift it and turn it over. Time this operation: time starts as the resist enters the water; turn it over after 7 to 10 seconds. After 20 seconds it will become limp; at about 30 to 35 seconds it will begin to bend backward.

The normal curve of the resist is inward toward the emulsion. As it wets the emulsion expands. This happens slowly in cold water. As the emulsion reaches maximum expansion (as noted by the paper trying gently to curl backward) the gelatin is very adhesive. This is the only time it will be! Remove the plate from the warm water and put it on a firm counter. Just as backward bending begins, lift the resist from the cold water and hold it face down over the copper plate. The resist is held by opposite ends and allowed to sag onto the warm copper plate. The middle touches first. The resist is swiftly and firmly squeegeed onto the plate with a Kodak blade squeegee. Excess water is immediately blotted from the backing paper, the edge of the plate, and the working area.

If the sequence is successful, the resist will adhere. Success will be evident in about two minutes as the backing paper begins to shrink. A good adhesion will not lift off. Poor adhesion will pull the resist away at the edge or in bubbles. There is nothing to do but begin again if this happens.

Test strips may be wetted in this way to practice and adhered to the white sheet of plexiglass, then developed.

DEVELOPING THE RESIST

The resist adheres to the support by natural adhesion. It must be allowed to dry until there is no feeling of dampness to the backing paper. This takes about 15 minutes. The gelatin shrinks and toughens.

Develop by immersing the plate in a tray of tap water at 80° *F*. Supply this tray with running water through a soft flexible hose. Rapidly raise the temperature of the water in the tray, lightly washing the back of the resist. Raise the temperature to 100 to 115° *F*. Do not exceed 120°. The hardened gelatin just under the backing paper will begin to melt at about 90° *F*.

After approximately a minute the plate will be obscured by white foam; tendrils of red molten gelatin will appear from the edges of the paper backing. Direct a stream of hot water along one edge of the tray and rock the tray steadily; spill about a fourth of the water with each rock. After another minute the backing paper should begin to lift. Stop rocking, grip the backing paper firmly, gently lift it. The unhardened gelatin between the image and the paper has softened, permitting the paper to separate from the resist. Throw away the paper.

If the paper is pulled away too rapidly, or if there are bubbles in the resist, some of the image will pull away.

If the adhesion is sound, the paper will release without damaging the image. All that can be seen is a cloudy mass of gelatin. Rock the tray; supply hot water along the edge of the tray, not onto the image area. Allow water to slop over the edge of the tray with each rock but be gentle. After four minutes the image will be clear. Continue developing for a total of ten minutes after paper removal. It is easy to leave a film of gelatin in the middle of the image and not see it. After six or seven minutes development the water should be clear.

After development turn off the hot water; leave the cold running. Rapidly bring down the water temperature to 60°—chilling gelatin and copper together. Keep rocking the tray. When the plate is cold, drain it, and stand it on edge to dry. Support it so that a puddle cannot form along the edge between the plate and the counter.

After two hours it is ready to etch.

If rosin is used for the ground, no alcohol can be used in development. If asphaltum is used, alcohol can be used to accelerate development and reduce wet-time. This is desirable: excessive hot water time sometimes causes blisters.

Inexpensive drugstore rubbing alcohol (about $0.15 a pint) is adequate for prewetting. After the resist has been adhered and dried, pour alcohol over the back of the paper. It will darken the paper. When water wets the resist backing it will penetrate more rapidly and accelerate the removal of emulsion between the paper and the image. After development, flush the image with alcohol; it will combine with water in the resist and dry it faster. A more even and controlled resist results. Alcohol cannot be used with rosin grounds.

ETCHING THE RESIST

Etching the gravure plate is not done with acid. Ferric Chloride is used because the large molecule migrates slowly through the resist. This chemical may be purchased as powder, and dissolved, or as a 48° Baumé solution. HUNT PHOTO CHEMICALS (with distributors in most large cities—they are suppliers of cine chemicals) provides Ferric Chloride in 50 lb. drums.

The 48° solution is very dense and must be watered for gravure etching. Solutions are needed in 2° intervals, from 38—44°. One way to dilute the stock is by using a hydrometer and adding water to two liters of concentrated etchant. Add 30-50ml at a time, stir and measure the specific gravity with a FISHER (Cat. No. 11-571E) hydrometer. When the desired concentration is reached, store that solution and begin again for the next.

An alternate mixing method is to use the following table, however the solutions mixed should be verified with the hydrometer.

To one liter of 48° Baumé etchant, add water as noted to achieve

46°	64.5 ml water	40°	302.5 ml water
44°	138	38°	394
42°	216		

ETCHING ROSIN GROUNDS

Prepare two plastic photo trays. They must be clean and completely dry. Pour about one-half inch of 48 degree etchant into one. In the second place an equal amount of 44 degree etching iron solution. Both solutions should be at 70° *F*.

The resist is frail when wet. A touch will mar it. To the back of the plate attach six-inch lengths of glass-fiber packaging tape. Fold an inch of the tape back on itself to make a holding tab. Attach one of these to each end. Using these tabs the plate can be lifted and agitated without fumbling. The etchant will not break down the adhesive on packaging tape.

Start the workroom timer with the first immersion. Immerse the plate in the 48 degree solution. Lift it immediately; gently squash bubbles. Agitate the plate by lifting and draining about every 15 seconds. At the end of two minutes transfer the plate to the 44 degree solution. The dense etchant conditions the gelatin. Some etching will take place in this solution. A darkening of the copper will show in Zone 0-II areas. Some etched copper precipitate will streak from these regions.

Return the 48 degree etch to its bottle.

Frequently lift the plate from the 44 degree etch and examine it. The worklight should be close to the tray. Light the tray so that as etching proceeds, small changes of color can be observed. Try to see when the first important shadow areas (Zones IV-V) change color. This is an indicator of total etching time. It should occur at 7 to 8 minutes.

A note on etching: All traditional literature on gravure etching speaks of using sequentially thinner baths—each 1 or 2 degrees less dense. McGraw Colorgraph research indicates that the traditions on which this etching system is based are in error. Traditional etching presupposed a necessity to begin etching tones at linear intervals. By moving the plate from a dense bath to a more watery one, more rapid penetration of the gelatin resist is achieved with quicker etching of higher Zones. McGraw Colorgraph discovered that for a given density range of the positive and with a given resist thickness (controlled by exposure) a single bath will produce smooth etching and greater separation of tones than will a multiple bath etching.

Single-bath etching is fine where variables can be controlled. In a school situation these cannot be controlled—and a compromise etching pattern is suggested.

After 12 minutes (if the plate has been etched this long) the highlights should have been penetrated. if not, a lower density bath must be used. Place the plate in a 42 degree solution. This should bring in the last tones within 60 seconds. If it does not, move the plate to a solution two degrees lower in density. The resist will begin to fail between 12 and 15 minutes.

When this happens the etchant will penetrate everywhere. When moving the plate to 42 and 40 degree solutions etching seems to "crawl" and colors flicker back and forth over the surface of the plate. Watch clear highlights closely for dark pinpoint penetrations. These are the first signs of penetration.

After etching is complete, clean the plate with water. This will destroy the gelatin resist. The rosin ground can be removed with alcohol.

ETCHING ASPHALTUM GROUNDS

The asphaltum particle is smaller and the gelatin conforms to it more tightly than with rosin. The resist for rosin ground can be more contrasty than for asphaltum, apparently because the looser conformation to the ground softens the image during etching.

Soak the plate in the 48 degree density solution for two minutes. Transfer the plate to a 44 degree bath. If the resist is of the right thickness (controlled by exposure) and the proper contrast (controlled by the positive), it will probably etch to completion, or nearly so, in this solution. If after 10 minutes the Zone VI values have not been penetrated, move the plate to a less dense solution.

A typical etching program using solutions of 2 degree Baumé intervals is:

44 B	(Zones 0-IV)	10 minutes
42 B	(Zones V-VII)	6 minutes
40 B	(if needed)	

Asphaltum ground melts at a high temperature. It is difficult to remove and may require some type of commercial tar-removing solution.

PREPARING THE GRAVURE COPPER PLATE

The copper plate must be prepared before exposing the resist. Use photoengraving sheet, prepared with an enamel resist on the reverse. A thin film of oil must be removed. The sheet of copper should be cut with the protective paper intact, to prevent scratching. Do not bevel the edges of the plate until etching is complete!

Degrease the plate using a warm solution of Sodium Hydroxide (50 grams in 1 liter of cool water). Scrub it with a cotton swab. CAUTION: *Wear rubber gloves.* Scrub the entire surface of the plate twice.

Dump the hydroxide. Flush the plate with hot tap water. Neutralize it with a solution of 1 part common salt, 1 part glacial acetic acid, and 10 parts water. Scrub the surface of the plate with this solution. Dump, flush with hot water, and then with distilled water. The plate should dry clear, without scum.

If a rosin ground is to be used, the plate may be silver coated. This protects the surface from oxidation. Dissolve ½ gram of Silver Nitrate in 1 liter of water. This will not dissolve fully. Add ½ gram of Potassium Cyanide to clear the mixture. Immerse the plate in this solution. Within 30 seconds a silver coating will appear on the copper. After 1½ minutes this is thick enough to protect the new copper surface but not thick enough to tear away under the tension of the gelatin resist.

Asphaltum grounds fire at a higher temperature where silver would be oxidized, so the copper is used bare. This affects the needed contrast of the resist. There is a copper-gelatin interaction creating a slightly tough surface layer. This reduces contrast.

Rosin dusting boxes are usually available where there are etching presses. Asphaltum dusting boxes can be easily built. The asphaltum powder is so finely pulverized that it need not be blown to provide a fine dust. A tumbling box at least 4 inches larger each way than the plate size, and 30 inches tall is adequate. A drawer near the bottom will provide an access for the plate and for recharging the box. A few teaspoons of asphaltum, three or four inversions of the box, and two dusting periods of 1½ to 2 minutes each will adequately coat the plate. The asphaltum can be fired with a butane torch if piped-in gas is not available. It is almost impossible to overfire the asphaltum. The dust does not melt, run, or varnish the plate as the rosin does. Fire the plate between successive dustings. A properly dusted plate is about 50% covered and 50% bare metal. Do not touch the surface of the plate after dusting.

Rosin is difficult to fire properly. When the silver-coated plate is removed from the dusting box the rosin granules are white. Place the copper on a heated plate used for inking and observe it. After 1-1½ minutes the rosin will melt. The granules change from white to pale yellow, then to a corn-oil yellow. Heated further, they lose shape and flow together, varnishing the plate. If this happens, clean it in oil-free alcohol and redust it. Examined under an 8-10 power loupe the correctly fired rosin particle will be separate, hemispherical, and golden in color.

Rosin is equivalent to a 120-line halftone screen. Asphaltum is equivalent to a 300-line screen. The advantage of both powders is that the screen is random—the eye of the observer cannot sense the mechanicalness of the screen.

INKING AND PRINTING THE GRAVURE PLATE

The final image tonal character is controlled by inking and printing. A standard etching ink may be too oily for a plate heated on an etching hotplate. A very stiff ink can be held by the shallow-etched gravure plate. If a low-temperature hotplate is used a very loose ink is better.

Rives BFK seems to have the best surface of contemporary printing papers. Soak it at least one hour before printing. The shallow image and the small dot pattern of the gravure plate interact unfavorably with other papers that have a chemical sizing.

Gravure plates can be printed on Japanese papers. These are not soaked but are laid directly on the plate and then backed by a damp piece of supporting paper, isolating the rice paper from the printing felts.

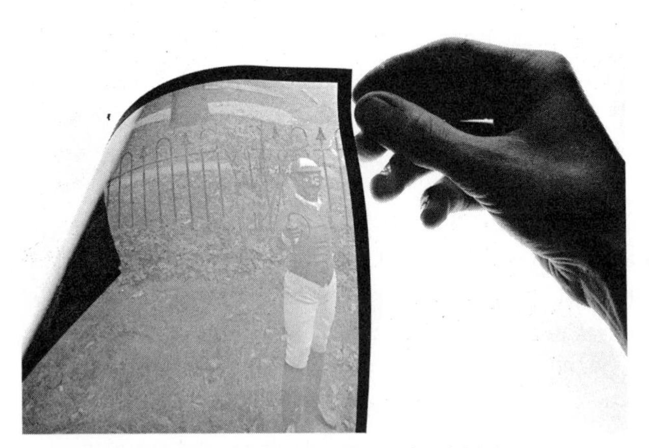

Fig. G-1: Gravure Positive by Transmitted Light

Fig G-2: Positive by Reflected Light

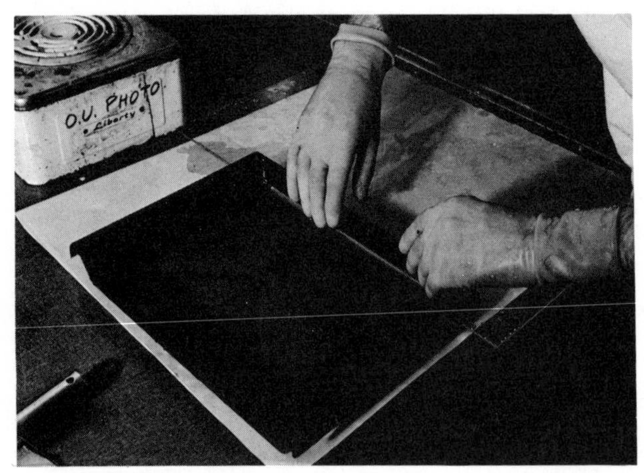

Fig. G-3: Sensitize Resist (note gloves)

Fig. G-4: Squeegee Resist onto Plexiglass

Fig. G-5: Test Plate Degreasing (note water tension)

Fig. G-6: Even Plate Wetting Indicates Degreasing

Fig G-7: Manual Application of Rosin Aquatint Ground

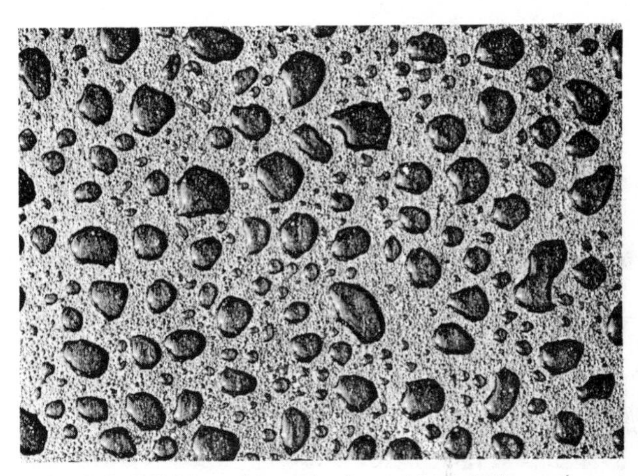

Fig G-8: 30X View of Aquatint Ground (app. 50% cover)

Fig. G-9: Place Swollen Resist Face Down on Plate

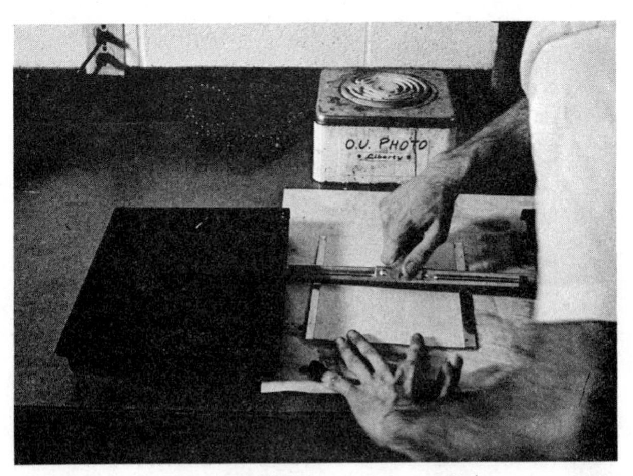

Fig. G-10: Squeegee Resist onto Aquatinted Plate

Fig. G-11: Blot Resist Dry and Surface Dry Resist

Fig. G-12: Start Development in Warm Water

Fig. G-13: Backing Paper Separates and is Lifted Away

Fig. G-14: Gelatin Foam Assists Washout of Image

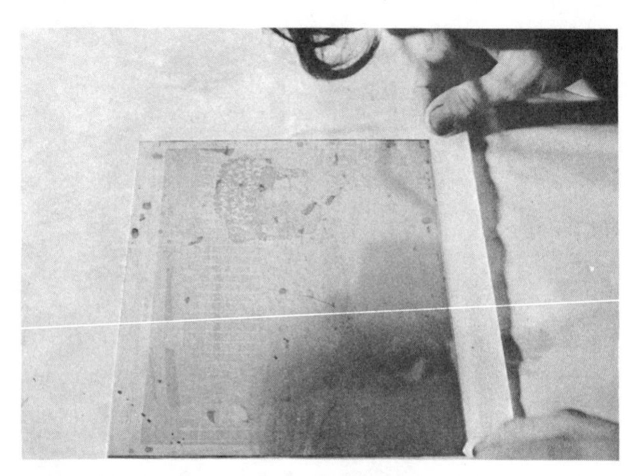

Fig. G-15: Mask Edges with 3M Tape before Etching

Fig G-16: Tape Straps Support Plate in Etchant

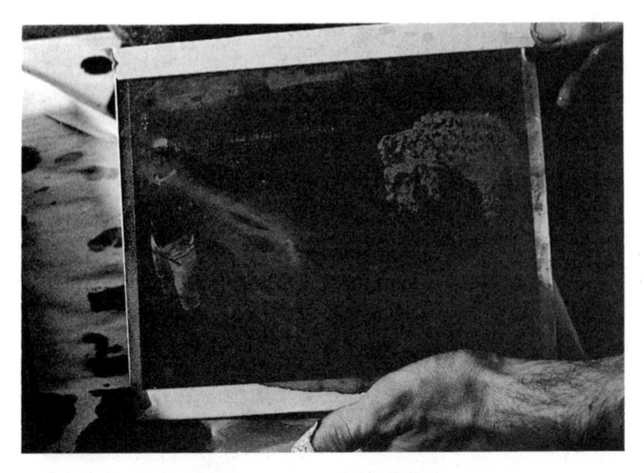

Fig G-17: Etched Plate Appears Dark & Brown

Fig G-18: Bevel Edges with File

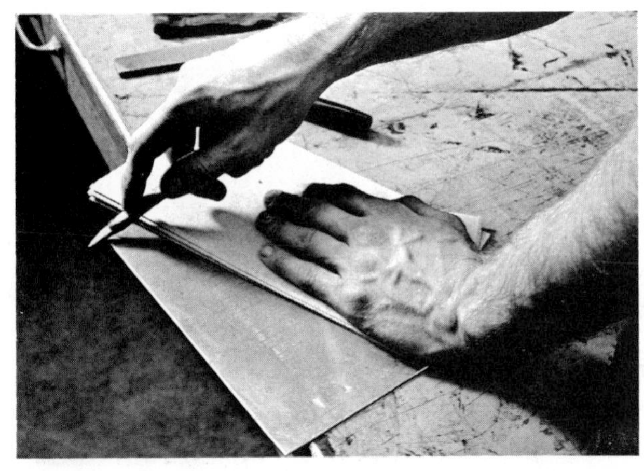

Fig G-19: Smooth Beveled Edges of Plate

Fig G-20: Heat Plate and Spread Ink Evenly

Fig G-21: Wipe Off Surface Ink with Tarleton

Fig G-22: Place Damp Printing Paper on Inked Plate

These illustrations of the steps of the gravure print process were prepared by A.J. Meek, who photographed the work of Eugene Groppetti.

Fig. G-23: After Rolling, Remove the Proof Print

PHOTO SILKSCREEN

The silk or nylon screen supports a gelatin resist made photographically. Images can be combined in the making of the resist or in printing the image.

Photosilkscreen resist is provided unsensitized or presensitized. The gelatin is made photosensitive by treatment with dichromate. It is, in fact, identical to gravure resist and is sold as "gravure and screen resist" by Chemco Corporation, Glen Cove, Long Island. The presensitized resist is also a gelatin but it is handled differently in development.

The unsensitized resist is placed face up in a tray of 3.5% Potassium Dichromate for 2 to 3 minutes. After soaking lay the tissue face down on a sheet of 0.003 inch acetate or mylar. Squeegee out excess fluid with a bar squeegee. Place the positive you wish to screen on the acetate sheet. The positive should appear in reversed position to how it should read in the finished print.

Expose the resist to blue or UV light. A mercury vapor lamp at 20 inches will require 3 to 8 minutes exposure. Overexposure will harden too much gelatin and adhesion will fail.

Separate the positive from the acetate and place the acetate face down on a smooth surface. Spray hot water onto the backing paper of the resist. The water should be between 100 and 115° *F*. After 20 to 30 seconds the backing paper will peel away. Continue washing the image with the spary until all unhardened gelatin has washed away and the water is clear. Quench the image in cold water.

Adhere the resist to the screen. Prepare the screen by scrubbing with an abrasive household cleanser (Ajax, Comet, etc.). Wet two cloth pads. Powder both with cleanser. Place a pad on each side of the screen; move them together and scrub the entire screen surface. Wash the screen. Neutralize with a 2% Acetic Acid solution. Place the resist, emulsion up, on a clean piece of masonite or plywood covered with a pad of newspaper. Three or four pieces of paper are sufficient. Position the clean damp screen over the resist. Lower it onto the resist and then place pieces of clean newsprint over the image and blot the image into the screen. After an hour the acetate can be peeled away. Liquid "blockout" should be applied to the screen around the image.

Presensitized material is exposed through the supporting sheet not through a cover sheet. The gelatin is then chemically hardened in a solution of Hydrogen Peroxide compounded from a proprietary developer solution. Development is 1½ to 2 minutes. After hardening, the image is washed out by hot water. If the image has been accidentally exposed on the emulsion side rather than through the transparent support, it will wash away in a scum. After development quench the image in cold water and adhere it.

Silkscreen requires a halftone image. Ink is pushed through holes in the resist by the squeegee blade. Halftone conversions are discussed earlier in the *Handbook.*

Fine halftones made from square-line screens (finer than 85 lines) can be printed without moire if the image is kept at an angle to the screen. It is not difficult to stretch the monofilament screen materials at a 15 to 30 degree angle to the screen and permit the image to be aligned parallel to the screen edges, and yet avoid moire.

The squeegee blade used for printing halftone or fine tone-line conversions should be "hard". Squeegee blades are supplied in three grades of hardness. The hard rubber or the plastic blade should be used. It makes a sharper image and requires less squeegee pressure. If drying ink begins to clog the screen, a commercial anti-drying agent (DRI-KILL) is available in aerosol cans. It is effective in opening the mesh without having to reclean the screen.

KALLITYPE PRINTS

Because of the steadily increasing cost of platinum and palladium during the past few years, the platinum print has become almost impossibly expensive for the student. The Kallitype process offers an image which has a surface resembling the platinum print, and a more straight-line response to the visual information of the negative than does the regular silver print, plus an image color that resembles the platinum print. Because it uses silver for the image, there is, however, the instability that is inherent in all silver-based prints.

The Kallitype process is in part a printing-out process, with a subsequent image development. Prints must be made by contact. Enlarged negatives can be made using the KODAK Professional Direct Duplicating Film (SO-015).

The final image is formed of metallic silver. The photosensitive emulsion is an iron salt. The salts used are those used for ferrocyanotype, but the sensitizer is compounded differently and only a faint image results from the direct exposure to light. The final image is created by adding silver nitrate to the print.

After being exposed with the negative to strong daylight, mercury vapor or arc light (for an exposure time similar to platinum) the print is immersed in a simple alkaline developer. Fixing is done in a weak sodium thiosulfate solution which has been buffered with ammonia.

The printing paper must be prepared by being sized, if a quality rag paper is being used. For first experiments a heavy bond typing paper may be used, without additional sizing being needed. For final prints on Arches, Reeves, Strathmore or other papers a starch sizing will be required (see Preparing Paper for Platinum Printing).

The sized paper is sensitized by spreading the photosensitive emulsion with a plastic brush. This may be done in weak tungsten light, but the paper must be dried in darkness. It is best to complete the drying with gentle heat before printing.

Kallitype Sensitizer:

Ferric Oxalate	5.0 grams
Oxalic Acid	0.3 grams
Water	30 ml

When the paper dries, warm it to complete the drying and expose immediately. A fully visible image will not be produced. Exposure is complete when the shadows are fully visible, but the print will be overexposed if detail appears in the middle tones or in the highlights. The image looks pale brown, against a yellow background. The following developers produce different image colors.

Kallitype Sepia Developer:

Potassium Sodium Tartrate	15 grams
Potassium Dichromate	0.1–0.3 grams[1]
Water	315 ml

Kallitype Cold-tone Developer:

Borax[2]	8 grams
Potassium Sodium Tartrate	30 grams
Potassium Dichromate	0.5 grams
Water	315 ml

Kallitype Black Developer:

Borax[2]	30 grams
Potassium Sodium Tartrate	22.5 grams
Potassium Dichromate	0.3–0.4 grams[1]
Water	315 ml

[1] *As with the platinum emulsions, increasing the amount of dichromate will increase both contrast and granularity.*
[2] *"Twenty Mule Team" Borax is sufficiently pure for this.*

Development may be done in weak tungsten light. A correctly exposed print cannot be over-developed. The image appears in a few seconds. Leave the print submersed in the developer for 5 minutes to be certain that full development has been obtained.

Wash the print for two minutes in running water following development. Fix it for 10 minutes in the following fixer:

Kallitype Fixing Solution:

Sodium Thiosulfate	50 grams
Ammonia (0.880 specific gravity)	12 ml
Water to make	1 liter

After the print is fixed, use a hypo elimination solution as directed for double-weight prints, and then wash thoroughly (as recommended for archival processing).

The print may be air dried or heat dried, and mounted by any standard method.

THE COLLOTYPE PRINT

Collotype is a halftone process. The print is an ink image. The halftone is very small, and the shape of the inked area is not a dot but a line. Because of this the collotype halftone pattern is very hard for the eye to resolve, and the sensation is of looking at a continuous-tone image. .The collotype has been used for reproduction of medical photography and copying of other art images because of this sense of continuous-tone reproduction is produces.

The collotype plate is a film of gelatin supported on glass (although grained zinc plates and even heavy plastic sheets have been used). A very fine pattern is produced in the gelatin by drying it rapidly; this causes the surface to reticulate, or to shrink unevenly, producing a net-work of interlocking ripplies.

The gelatin used will produce an image whose contrast and fineness of halftone pattern both vary according to the "hardness" or "Bloom" of the gelatin used. Older texts refer to hardness, specifying a hard or medium gelatin for collotype printing. A standard testing method is now used to determine the Bloom index which is a measure of the resilience and resistance to penetration of the gelatin under force which is less than that required to rupture the mass.

The gelatin used should be in the range of 150-240 Bloom. Knox (food grade) Gelatin falls midway in this range. Whatever gelatin is used, enough should be obtained to carry through a complete series of testing and printing because the source of the gelatin (in terms of bone or skin) affects the nature of the pattern of the reticulation and the ink/water interactions that result in the print.

The photosensitivity of the gelatin is produced by using Potassium or Ammonium Dichromate. This is added to the gelatin as part of the liquid used to dissolve the colloid. When the reticulated gelatin is exposed to a continuous-tone negative, the ability of the gelatin to swell and absorb water is reduced by interaction of the light, the dichromate and the gelatin's molecular structure. The net effect is that where there has been exposure to light the gelatin becomes less absorbent of water. Because it will remain "unwetted" when the whole surface has been subjected to wetting, the exposed areas will then accept ink, whereas the unexposed areas (swollen and full of water) will reject ink.

Collotype is then a planographic printing process which closely resembles stone lithography, and some of the terminology and most of the techniques of lithographic printing are used for collotype, although the essential image making is photographic.

SPECIAL EQUIPMENT NEEDED

1. 91 mm Buchner funnel (Fisher 10-356D)
2. 500-ml Filtering flask (Fisher 10-180E)
3. No. 5, one-hole stopper for filtering flask
4. 500-ml Erlenmeyer flask (2) (Fisher 10-039F)
5. No. 5 stoppers for Erlenmeyer flasks
6. 9 cm filters (Fisher 9-795C)
7. Aspirator (Fisher 9-956) and threaded adaptor (Fisher 9-975B)
8. 5 feet ¼" rubber tubing for aspirator
9. Collotype Oven. The oven is a box made of three-quarter inch plywood. A useful size is 18" x 24" x 16" high. The top is not flat, but slopes 2-4 inches. The oven is electrically heated. An easy way to heat it is to use the heating tapes made for protecting pipes from freezing. 200-400 watts of heating tape is needed. In a warm climate less will be needed.

The temperature of the box must be controlled and set at 120° F. A precision thermoregulator is FISHER Scientific Company Cat. No. 15-178. However a standard electrical baseboard heater thermostat may be used, provided the element is bent slightly to cover the temperature range needed. A manual control can be made by supplying electricity to the tape through a light-dimming SCR switch, of the kind available in most hardware stores, made for residential use. Figure C-1 shows a collotype oven with the cover removed (and without a heat dispersion plate). The heating tape is seen at the bottom. Halfway between the tape and the glass collotype plate should be a sheet of aluminum (of the sort sold in most hardware stores). The aluminum heat dispersing plate prevents currents of hot air from circulating and averages the internal temperature of the oven.

The collotype plate is supported midway between the heat dispersing plate and the top of the box. Supports are metal anglestock which has been drilled and tapped to accept 12/24 screws. The screws are the actual support of the glass, permitting each plate to be individually leveled in place. The location, and number of screws, will depend on the size of plates and the number desired at one time. Heavy angle should be used because the plate glass will deform light-weight stock and the glass will become unlevel during curing, causing printing problems.

The lid can be solid, with a number of 1½-2″ diameter holes, or it can be a frame which supports a piece of canvas (for strength) and a piece of black linen or nylon (for light-tightness). In the first case, the holes must be covered by black lintless cloth to keep light from the plate during curing.

The lid is sloped to prevent condensation from dripping back onto the plates. The minimum slope is 1″ in 12″. The oven should be placed on a very solid support, away from casual traffic, so the plates can cure without being disturbed.

10. Precision Level: to level the glass plates for coating and drying.
11. Lithographic printing supplies:
    Composition roller, support, and cuffs.
    Lithographic inks (black or process colors)
    Potassium Carbonate, reducing oil, spatula, rollup slab, Lithotene, etc.
12. Flat Press, with felts to control pressure
13. Waxed Paper and "Goldenrod" paper for masking
14. 500 grams of granular skin gelatin (150-240 Bloom)
15. 500 grams of Ammonium or Potassium Dichromate
16. 1 liter Sodium Silicate
17. 500 grams Alum
18. 1 liter Glycerine (= Glycerol)

PREPARING THE PLATE

Grain the surface of the plate glass by grinding it with a lithographic levigator, or lay it on a lithographic stone and use another stone as the grinding surface. Use 320 mesh Carborundum. A fine even tooth is desired. It need not be deep, but must be uniform.

Coat the plate with Substratum and set it aside to dry. Heat the oven.

Level the dry plate in the oven and then heat the oven and plate to 120° F.

Weigh out the correct amount of gelatin (Figure C-4) for the plate and add the amount of cold water indicated in the table below. Allow the gelatin to swell for at least 20 minutes (problems with image irregularities often stem from insufficient swelling time). Heat the gelatin and water to 110-115° F. Add the correct amount of Dichromate sensitizer and then filter through paper, using the Buchner funnel assisted by an aspirator (see Section 4 Titlepage illustration). Stir gently; allowing bubbles to be absorbed but maintain the gelatin temperature in a water bath. Pour the gelatin onto the leveled glass plate (see Figure C-5) which has been prewarmed in the oven. Spread the emulsion evenly. Cover the collotype oven. Bake the plate for four hours until hard and dry to the touch. The plate may be exposed immediately.

Prepare the negative for printing by masking out the area surrounding the image with opaque paper (the yellow paper used by printers called "goldenrod" is economical and lintfree).

Place the negative on the plate. Remember the image will print reversed left-to-right. Cover the negative with a piece of glass to hold the negative and plate smoothly together and expose to electric arc, mercury vapor, or sunlight. For initial tests try 4 minutes at 18 inches from a standard NUMADE arc light.

The plate is "developed" by soaking it in clear water between 55-60° F. This washes out the Dichromate but does not allow excessive swelling of the gelatin (which appears as coarsened image detail and loss of highlight separations). Soak the plate for 10 minutes and then drain (Figure C-6), and then repeat at 30 minute intervals until both water and plate are clear of any yellow Dichromate stain.

Dry the plate completely before beginning printing from it.

PRINTING THE COLLOTYPE PLATE

The collotype plate is prepared for printing by being "etched". This term is a carryover from engraving, just as "development" (the washing out of the Dichromate sensitizer) is a carryover from photographic printmaking. "Etching" means wetting the surface of the gelatin, preparing it for the printing ink.

The contrast of the image is affected in part by the pH of the gelatin. The gelatin can be made to swell and become more absorbent (relative to the exposed and hardened areas) by adding a few drops of ammonia solution to the etchant. However, the ink will not adhere in the presence of ammonia. If ammonia is used in the etchant to increase contrast, that etching solution must be washed away by flowing a neutral etchant (glycerine and water only) onto the plate. This is mopped off before inking.

The 3:2 ratio for etchant is a starting point. Individual plates, and variations in ink, will require adjustments. More glycerine in the etchant will permit more ink to adhere. More water will reduce the amount of ink taken by the plate. When the balance for a particular plate/ink combination is discovered it should be recorded and used again for that plate the next time it is printed.

While the plate is being etched, prepare the lithographic ink. Standard lithographic printing inks will work. Contrast is controllable in part by stiffening the ink with Potassium Carbonate.

The stiffer the ink, the higher the contrast (see Figure C-7). If the ink becomes too stiff it may be eased by the addition of a reducing oil.

When the ink has been spread on the rollup slab and rolled into a thin, smooth layer, begin rolling up the plate. Roll very slowly, with light pressure (Figure C-8). The collotype image is much more sensitive to rolling speed and pressure than the lithographic stone or plate. Roll up slowly and if there is overinking, remove ink with quick, light rolling. Ink roller speed will control how much ink is taken by the plate; the plate may be rolled almost completely clean by very fast rolling.

The unexposed areas outside the image will always accept some ink. To keep the margins completely white it is necessary to mask them physically, after inking, for each impression. This is done by using strips of wax paper (Figure C-10). The wax paper also prevents the paper fibers from sticking to the slightly tacky gelatin where it is unprotected by ink.

Like all lithographic prints, the collotype plate does not print repeatably until several prints have been inked and pulled (Figure C-9). Allow five or six impressions to be made before attempting to judge tonality, contrast, or inking technique.

COLLOTYPE SOLUTIONS

Plate Substratum

A.	Gelatin	3 grams
	Water	100 ml
B.	Alum	1 gram
	Water	100 ml

Soak the gelatin for 20-30 minutes, then heat it gently until it becomes liquid, but not past 130° F. Warm the Alum solution (B) to 120° F, and combine parts A and B. Add 20 ml Sodium Silicate. Filter with the Buchner funnel and store in a tightly stoppered bottle until needed.

Collotype Sensitizer

Ammonium Dichromate	3.5 grams
Water	120 ml

Potassium Dichromate may also be used. The negative exposure will be increased about 2X to produce the same image density. There are also differences in grain structure produced by the two Dichromates.

Collotype Developing

Plain water is used. The temperature is important. Temperatures above 60° cause coarse grain.

COLLOTYPE DEFECTS

wave patterns in image	temperature variations in oven
blisters, airbells in emulsion	unclean plate, improper substratum, grease, dust.
mottled image	gelatin too thick, plate unlevel during drying, temperature too low during drying, temperature uneven in oven
plate breaks down	inadequate exposure
overall greyness	too little ink rolled up, negative density range inadequate
muddy highlights, overall flatness	"continuing action" (characteristic of all dichromate sensitized emulsions) of gelatin caused by excessive delay between drying and exposure, or exposure and washout or both. This is reinforced by high temperature/humidity combinations in workroom. Also caused by low oven temperature during curing of gelatin.
scumming	insufficient etching time, or dry plate. A commercial lithographic "fountain" solution may be of assistance.

CALCULATING EMULSION QUANTITIES

Plate Size (inches)	Plate Area (square inches)	Gelatin (grams)	Water (ml)	Sensitizer (ml)	Total Volume[1,2] (ml)
8 x 10	80	2	32	8	40
10 x 12	120	3	48	12	60
11 x 14	154	3.85	61.5	15.5	77
16 x 20	320	8	128	32	160

[1]add 4 ml of water to the volume of emulsion mixed to allow for loss in transferring and and filtering.

[2]the general rules for calculating the emulsion needed are:

(1) 0.0625 grams of gelatin for each milliliter of fluid
(2) ratio of water to dissolve gelatin to sensitizer is 4:1
(3) ½ml of sensitized emulsion is needed for each square inch of plate surface

A note on gelatin: The Bloom index has different correlations to viscosity and the reticulation characteristics of an emulsion depending on the source of the gelatin. Photographic gelatins are made from "limed" (i.e. bone or calfskin sources) gelatin. This gelatin has been largely supplanted in food gelatins by porkskin (acid) gelatins which have different physical properties. Sources for calfskin gelatin are KIND & KNOX, Suite 300, 900 Kings highway, Cherry Hills, New Jersey 08034; and U.S. GELATIN, div. Peter-Cooper, Oak Creek, Wisconsin, as well as most scientific supply houses, but care must be taken to specify calfskin or neutral gelatin.

Figure C-1: Collotype Oven

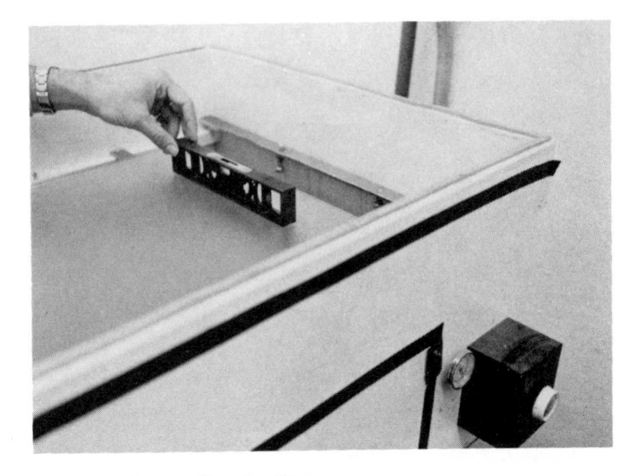

Figure C-2: Leveling the Plate

Figure C-3: Masked Separation Negative

Figure C-4: Measuring Gelatin for 16x20 in. Plate

Figure C-5: Spreading the Gelatin on Warm Plate

Figure C-6: Plate During Development

Figure C-7: Mixing Ink with Carbonate

Figure C-8: Rolling Ink on Collotype Plate

Figure C-9: Pulling a Proof

Figure C-10: Masking White Edges with Wax Paper

Collotype, like gravure printing, is dependent on the precise repeatability of conditioning the gelatin reticulated surface (or etching resist, in the case of gravure), and this in turn means having constant humidity and temperature conditions. If these are not available, if there is neither humidity nor temperature controls for the room in which the collotype oven is operated, there there will inevitably be variations in reticulation size, and in contrast and image printing characteristics from one plate-making session to the next.

quick-drying blockout liquid is spread on screen to maintain white print borders. photo: D. James Dee

5: color prints

COLOR PRINTS

Color imposes new disciplines upon the photographer, especially if he is concerned with either naturalistic color or repeatable results. All simple color print methods involve separating the image into three layers. These are printed in pigments or dyes of magenta, cyan and yellow colors. See Figure 5-1.

Separations of these colors can be made from the original subject, from a color transparency, or mechanically provided by a color negative.

The printing materials can be dyes formed chemically in photographic paper, gum layers applied and exposed sequentially in register, or photosilkscreens printed sequentially in register. There are other methods: conventional film positives can be made, then dyed and registered; or photogravure plates made from separations and sequentially printed. Once any one system is understood and mastered, its disciplines will carry over into the other processes.

SEPARATION NEGATIVES

These can be made from the subject, exposing directly onto black and white film through primary filters, or be made from a color photograph. A color negative has the separation images already provided in three layers supported in register.

Making separations from the original subject requires a sturdy tripod and gentle handling of the filmholders. One negative is exposed through a Wratten A filter. A second is exposed through a Wratten B filter. A third through a Wratten C-5 filter. The filter factor for each of these is eight times the metered exposure (or three stops). The development for each film will differ. The red (A) filter requires about 70% as much development as the green (B) filter, and the blue (C-5) requires about 120-130% as much development as the green-filter negative. This is because the red image tends to be more contrasty and the blue less contrasty than the green-filtered image.

Separation from a transparency is more common. This is described in an Eastman Kodak book: *Separation Negatives from Color Transparencies*; and also in Section 16 of the Photo Lab Index.

Super-XX film is still the best film available for separations. Other panchromatic films will work but they all seem to have nonlinear responses. They cause color shifts when the images are brought together in register as a color (rather than a density) statement.

A correct separation negative for any of the following processes looks dense when compared with a conventional projection or contact printing negative. The areas of maximum density in the transparency (black) should have a definite density in the separation. This places the least important shadow detail fully at a Zone IV density when compared to a conventional negative. This is an area of linear response, causing the least distortion of tones in the transfer from a silver image to a silver image. If the separation had 'normal' shadow densities the final image would be grossly distorted, with crushed separation of shadow tones.

SEPARATION FROM 35mm TRANSPARENCIES (FOR GUM PRINTING)

Enlarger at *f*5.6; enlargement ratio set to produce a 3½ inch image from the length of the full 35mm frame. Use Wratten gelatin filters #29, 61, 47B sequentially. These can be placed on the variable contrast filter support just before the lens. They are so thin they will not affect focus. Film: Super-XX sheet.

	Red	Green	Blue
Exposure:	14''	8''	6''
Development:	4'	3'36''	7'12''

Develop the film in HC-110 diluted 1:64, at 70 degrees F. The simplest way to insure evenly developed film is: develop all three sheets at the same time in the same tray. One-half ounce of HC-110 and 32 ounces of water are used. Mix them just before developing.

Expose the film in a paper easel, or use film-holders to support it until ready for development. Identify the red sheet by leaving it whole; clip a corner of the green; and two corners of the blue. This way they can be identified in the dark.

One at a time immerse the sheets of film in the developer. The blue sheet should go in first. Place it face down, immediately turn it over face up, and then turn it back face down. Place the green sheet in next, and repeat the movement over and back. Immerse the red sheet: down, up, down. With the left hand span the film gently to hold it in place. With the right hand pull the bottom sheet out, then lay it on top of the stack. Repeat with the green sheet, then the red.

It will take about five seconds exactly to immerse each sheet. If the clock has been set for 7' 12'' when you started, then note when 3'41'' have elapsed and pull the second (green) sheet. When 4' 10'' have elapsed, remove the third (red) sheet. Every 20 seconds lift, drain, and replace the blue sheet until the time runs out.

A correct negative will have densities of about 0.30 produced by the black areas of the transparency. The first visible shadow details of the transparency will have a density of about 0.35. Highlights with texture will have densities of about 0.90 to 1.00.

The negatives made for gum separations are also ideal for the photosilkscreen images described later.

PRINTING GUM SEPARATIONS

The controls needed for naturalistic rendering are more severe than for monochromatic gum. The paper must be sized twice and hardened thoroughly. Yellow is printed first. This image (and also the magenta) is easy to control and develop. Cyan is printed last and is more difficult. Print the cyan in two layers for good results. Yellow cannot be printed last because the color saturates the gelatin that by this time is becoming softer and more absorbent.

The most successful colors are WINDSOR and NEWTON. The #5 tube is economical but few suppliers carry it. For three color printing the following approximate 'process' colors:

cyan:	use Windsor blue. Mix 1 g color with 13 ml water.
magenta:	use Alizarin Crimson. Mix 1 g color with 10 ml water.
yellow:	use Cadmium yellow. Mix 1 g color with 12 ml water.

The exposure can be made using a two-tube desk model fluorescent light, set at 12 inches from the contact print frame. Exposure will take about 25 minutes. Develop by inspection in 70 degree F water.

The gum is best applied by using a wide polyfoam brush; this type of brush is now commonly available. It spreads the gum smoothly and easily without streaking or damaging the under layers.

MAKING PHOTOSILKSCREEN HALFTONE COLOR PRINTS

There are two ways to make separations for photosilkscreen halftone color prints. Separations may be made from a transparency or from a color negative.

For the whole process the assumption is that naturalistic rendering is not being attempted at first. A color print will result which may require trial-and-error reworking of inks (and possibly separation prints and halftone negatives) but which is nevertheless a useful tool to the creative printmaker.

Photosilkscreen halftone images may be made without the use of a process camera. Halftone negative manufacturing services may be purchased from a commercial photoengraver or halftone negatives may be made by the photographer using KODAK AUTOSCREEN film.

Autoscreen film is a high contrast photoengraving film. It has been pre-exposed to a 133-line dot pattern and bears the latent screen image. When a second exposure is added to the latent image of the screen it automatically creates a halftone image. No external screen is needed. Halftone negatives can be made with any view camera.

The screen dot pattern is too fine to use directly on silkscreens. This is an advantage; halftone negatives can be made on 4×5 in film, and then enlarged to produce a coarser dot pattern. Since a positive image is required for exposing the screen resist material, this is an economical sequence.

POSITIVES FROM SEPARATION NEGATIVES

It is possible to make separation halftones directly from a color transparency or print. This requires complete control of a process camera. It is more economical and practical for a school or private lab to make separation negatives on Super-XX or other film, then separation prints on regular silver printing paper. From these, halftone negatives can be made, with screen patterns lying in different directions, and then halftone positives. The positives are contact printed onto screen resists. These are adhered to screens and then inks are screened in register onto the paper. Figure 5-2 illustrates the entire sequence.

Separation positives are conventional silver prints made from separation negatives. They are low in contrast and have a limited tonal range (similar to negatives) to reduce color distortion. To make the positive, place the green separation negative in the enlarger. It most resembles a 'normal' negative. Set the enlarger for an image area that fits into an 8×10 inch format with at least half-inch borders on all sides. Make a trial exposure on Agfa 3 Brovira 111, and develop it in Metinol U, diluted 1:3, for 1′ 30″. Hold the developer at 70 degrees F. Develop by clock, with constant agitation. The most repeatable agitation is to immerse the print, then lift it and lay it back in the developer. Repeat this slowly for the whole development time.

The print should appear very grey and with full detail in both shadows and highlights. At best it should look like a weak 'drugstore' print, with no hard blacks, and definite tone separation throughout.

Do not change the exposure or disturb the enlarger settings. Once proper exposure for the green negative is established, use this for all negatives. Mark the prints as you expose them so they can be identified later. Develop all three prints together. Immerse the first, lift it

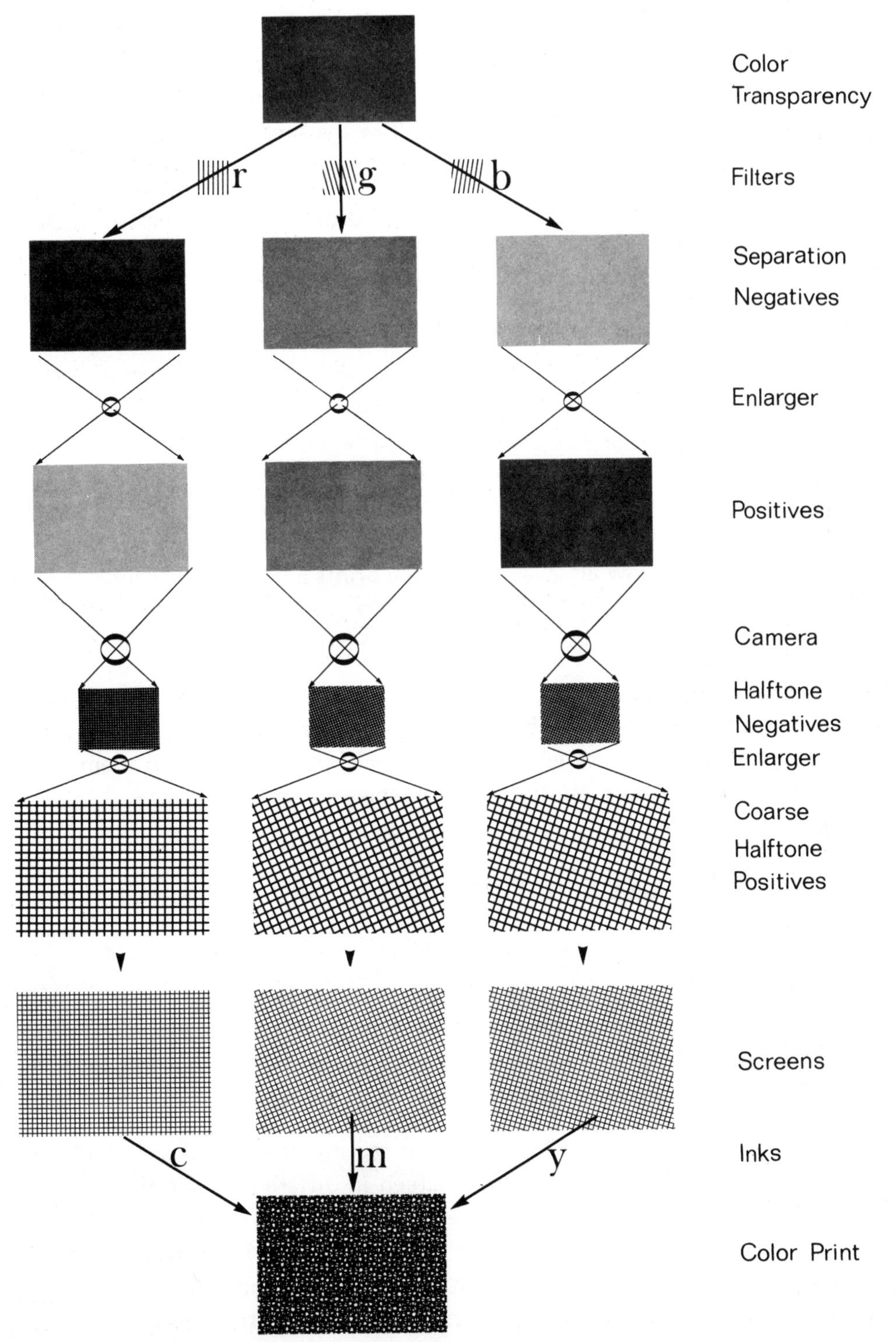

FIGURE 5·2 three color screen process

and replace it. Push it to the bottom of the tray. Immerse the second: lift, drain, and replace. Immerse the third. Then agitate them, pulling the bottom print out and placing it on top of the stack. It will take about 5 seconds to carefully wet each print. Keep track of which print you are handling. When 1'30" has elapsed, withdraw the first print and place it in a stop bath. Five seconds later pull the second print. Pull the third five seconds after the second print.

Fix them normally in the fixing bath in the same order they were placed in the developer. Rotate them in the fixing bath in the same way they were rotated in the developer. When they are fixed then neutralize, wash, and dry the prints.

Dry these prints on a drying rack. Do not attempt to dry them with heat. A drying rack is a wooden frame with a nylon mesh stretched over it. A frame of screen door stock with nylon window screening may be used, or it may be covered more cheaply with nylon bobbinette. The latter is obtainable from a tent-and-awning supply house. After the print is washed, drain it on a smooth clean tilted surface. Allow it to drain until it loses its wet look. Then place the print face down on the drying rack. A doubleweight print will dry in about three hours. Do not point an electric fan directly at the prints; drying may be accelerated by using a fan but direct it above the rack to blow air away. When the prints are dry they will be smooth and curl a bit. Flatten them by placing them face down on a piece of clean mount board. Close them in a dry mounting press heated to 175 degrees F. Flatten them for 5 to 10 seconds. Store them under a light weight.

Prints produced in this way will be within 1/100 inch register tolerance in both major axes and will remain in register as long as they are stored together. Do not keep them under pressure where only the edges can absorb moisture. Store separation prints in sets.

HALFTONE NEGATIVES FROM SEPARATION PRINTS

Halftone negatives can be made with an ordinary view camera using Kodak Autoscreen film; or with a process camera, photoengraving film and glass screens, magenta or grey contact screens. If someone other than yourself is going to make the halftone negatives they can be prepared for the camera in such a way that work is minimized.

Because three halftone images will be printed in register it is necessary to place the screen patterns caused by the halftone dot-forming screen in different directions. This permits the patterns to overlap and not create a major new pattern called *moire*. The angle of separation between one pattern and the next should be between 20 and 40 degrees. Prepare the prints for separation negative making by mounting them as shown in Figure 5-3. When they are taken to the engraver (a local newspaper or small job printer) tell him to make the negatives

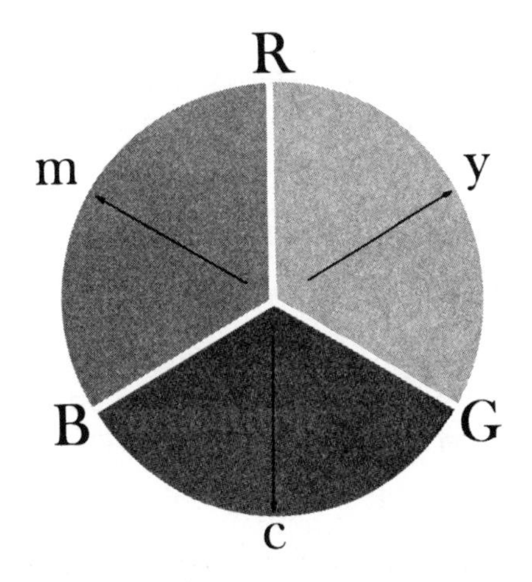

FIGURE 5·1 photographic primary colors

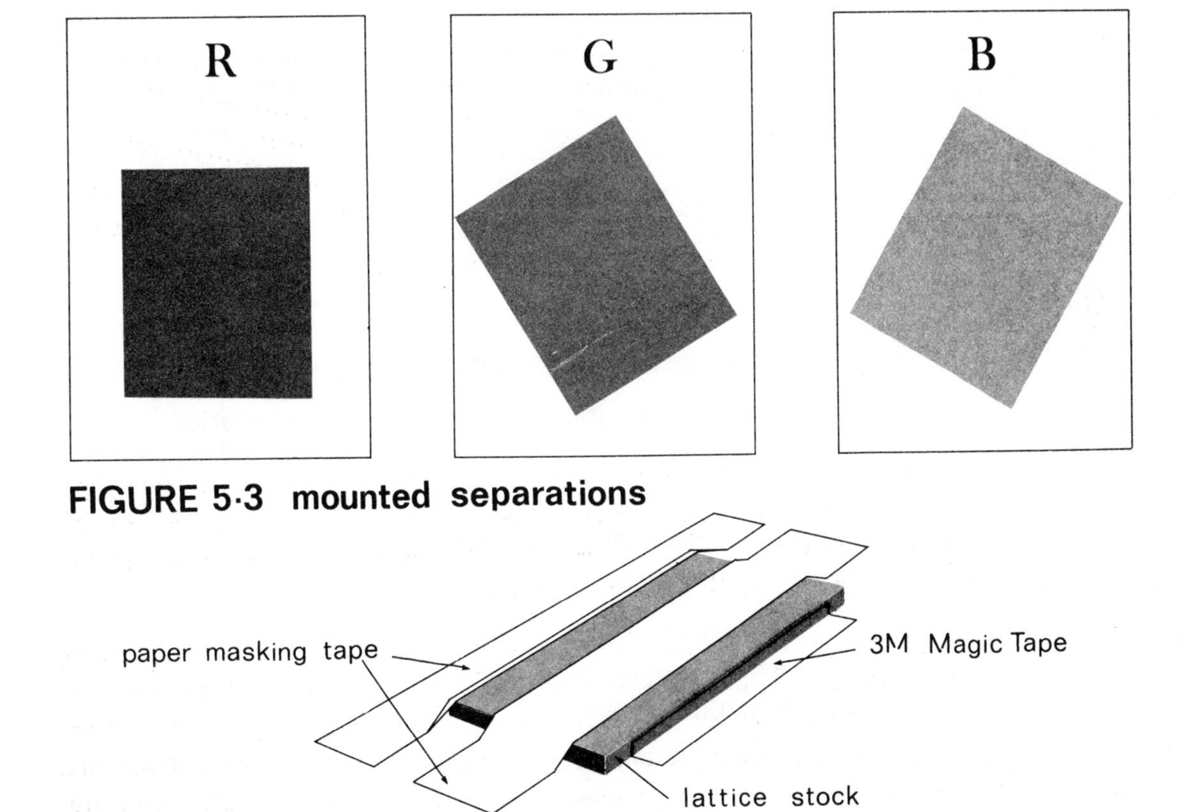

FIGURE 5·3 mounted separations

FIGURE 5·4 screen register block

with all the mounts vertical. This will ensure that the halftone dot patterns have the correct angles. If you wish to make the halftones yourself, you may do so with Autoscreen film. Use a viewcamera to photograph your positives. The information with the film provides the necessary information on exposure-density control.

The halftone negative you desire is one which looks like a conventional negative. The negative image size is controlled by the screen dot size you desire in the final image.

A very coarse screen can be used in three-color photosilkscreen image making without making a coarse looking image. This is because the three images overlap, transparent inks are used, and each image has a pattern with a differently directed axis. This combination largely destroys the granularity of the screen. A 60-line-per-inch screen image is not objectionable in three-color printing.

If the final image size you desire is, for example, 8″ across, and a 60-line screen is desired, then from a 133-line negative, your negative image will have to be 3-5/8″ across. In a working formula this can be expressed:

$$\frac{\text{negative screen}}{\text{print screen}} = \frac{\text{screened image size}}{\text{negative image size}}$$

In this example:

$$\frac{133}{60} = \frac{8}{\text{negative image size}}$$

and:

negative size = 8 (60/133) = 3.6 or 3-5/8 inches.

Coarser screens can be used; they will then be a noticeable part of the image esthetics.

The halftone negatives should be made on dimensionally stable film for ease of registration. After the halftone negatives are dry, enlarge them to finish size. Be careful not to change the enlarger settings and to keep the same processing conditions throughout.

Enlarge the negatives onto a conventional high-contrast photoengravers film. Process it normally, fix, wash, and dry. If the film is not on a mylar base, be certain that all the positives are hung from the same corner of the image to avoid differences in axial deformation.

Place the red-separation positive emulsion down on a light table or a large piece of glass. Tape it at two corners with Scotch Magic Mending tape. Place the green-separation positive over this. Move it until the image is in exact register, then tape it in place. Register the blue-positive halftone over the other two. The separate images seem incomplete and 'wrong' but when registered they assume a tonal strength and a sense of completeness and the image sharpness improves. Separate positives look thin and unsharp.

Trim the positives in register. Place a metal straightedge along the edge of the image. With a matt knife make a straight vertical cut through the stacked positives. Expose silkscreen resists from each positive and adhere them to screens. Block out and print.

PRINTING THREE-COLOR PHOTOSILKSCREENS

Standard "process" colors are dependable starting places for three-color separation printing with silkscreen images. The colors need to be calibrated for balance. Make a screen by exposing a ZIP-A-TONE 93 halftone screen pattern onto a resist and transferring that to a screen. This pattern is a density wedge, from light to dark (or from small dots to large ones).

Mix trial batches of process red, blue and green inks. Process inks are normally printed in a a yellow-red-blue sequence, but this may be reversed for ease of color balance.
If the yellow is to be screened last, then a trial batch of inks could be mixed:

Blue	40 grams	Halftone Base	500 grams
Red	40-80 grams†	Halftone Base	500 grams
Yellow	10 grams*	Halftone Base	500 grams

†If "permanent Process" red is used the larger volume is needed.
*If the yellow were screened first, the amount would be larger.

Use the same screen for all three colors. Screen 10 prints with the trial Blue Mixture. Dry them. Screen five with the trial Red mixture, having offset the dots (misregister) about a half-dot off. Then, offsetting the screen image again, in the opposite direction, screen the third color, yellow onto the first two.

Study the colors produced. A perfect balance of primaries will produce a passable grey, shading from light to dark. Too much yellow will cause a green cast (or, conversely, too little red, which is really a summation of red + blue). If the colors are all too dense, the nominal grey wedge produced will be dark; if they are too thin, the wedge will be pastel. Remix the red and yellow to adjust for the conditions noted in the first five prints, and screen the other five, to verify your prediction.

With balanced inks, minor variations in separation negatives and in halftone conversions can be accomodated by simply varying the weight of ink used in a given quantity of base.

Registration of the second screen is achieved by moving registration blocks, if inexpensive clamp hinges are used that do not permit registration changes. Figure 5-4 shows a useful registration block made from a 3" strip of wood lattice stock, cut and sanded. Use three of these, two on the long and one on the short side. Register the screen visually to the cyan printing, then tape the registration block in place with three strips of tape. A piece of masking tape over the top, to hold it down; one across the back edge and onto the table to prevent it sliding away; and a strip of Magic Mending Tape across the inner edge and onto the table to prevent the printing paper from catching on the bottom of the wood.

Examine the finished product. If necessary any one of the screens can be re-used to screen a primary again or to screen a modifying color. Sometimes the entire print needs to be darkened by adding all three primaries. Sometimes only one needs modification. An overall red image can be helped by running the cyan screen again with a green-enriched ink. The logic of the color wheel of Figure 5-1 can be examined and extended as shown in Figure 5-5.

Adding yellow will diminish all colors that lie below the marked diameter; this will darken the blue most and have lesser effects on magenta and greens. Adding magenta will darken green most and change cyan and yellow to some extent. Adding cyan will darken red most and effect magenta and yellow to some degree.

SEPARATION POSITIVES FROM COLOR NEGATIVES

Color negatives can be used directly to make separation positives. GAF Panchromatic paper is good for this purpose. The paper is not equally sensitive to all colors of light. For a given emulsion make a test by placing a KODAK Uncalibrated Step Wedge in the enlarger. Place a piece of unexposed, developed, clear orange base color negative in the film carriage. Handling the paper in total darkness, expose test strips of the paper to red, green, and blue. Develop them in Metinol U (diluted 1:4) at 70 degrees F for 1½ minutes. By trial and error bring them to balance. Fortunately the paper does not need different developing times (as does film separating) but does need different quantities of light for each of the primaries. After determining balanced exposures, replace the grey scale and blank sheet of film with a regular color negative. Make separation positives directly and proceed to a print. The GAF paper has a brown-black image color. This means, in terms of the sensitivity of the halftone film, that all shadow values must be placed high, that is, be kept 'grey', or they will drop out in making halftones.

THREE-COLOR PRINTING WITH CONVENTIONAL COLOR PAPERS

The same filters used for making separation negatives can be used for printing chemical color prints and these are the only filters needed. With AGFA color print paper (MCN 111) and the recommended Agfa chemistry, it is possible to print color in any normally equipped darkroom. No other equipment is needed.

The solutions are made so that they survive tray operation. Agfa literature indicates that a gallon of paper developer is useful for about fifty 8×10 inch prints. The solution can be used about 30% more if repeatable color is not needed.

FIGURE 5·5 primary subtractive colors

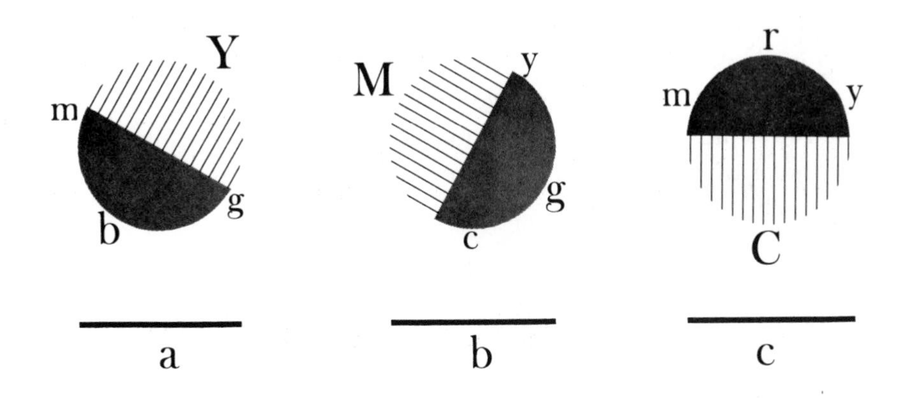

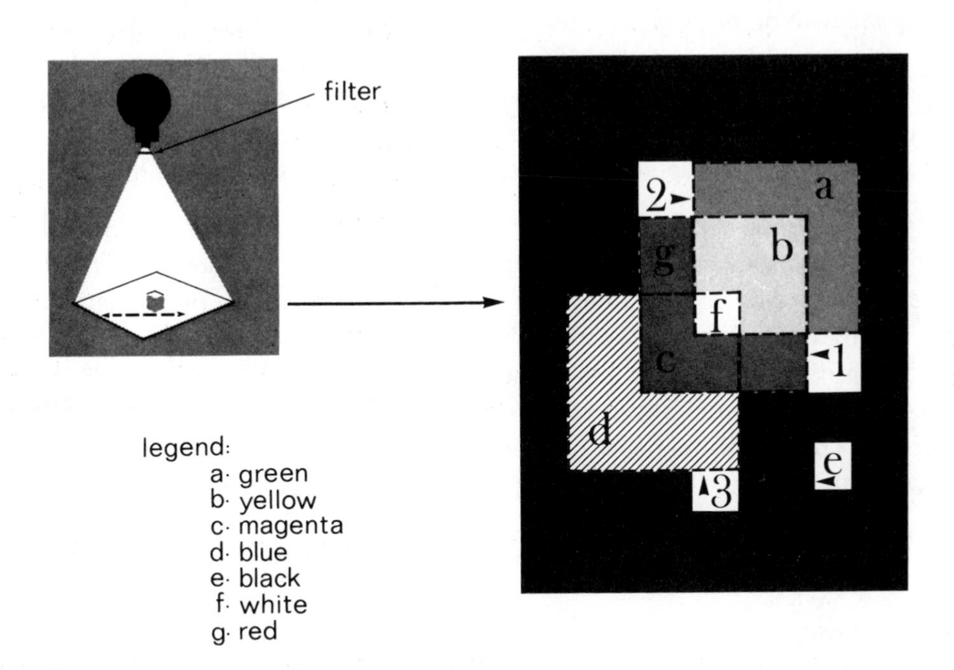

FIGURE 5·6 basic color demonstration

The tray line is almost the same as that for conventional printing: developer, running-water rinse (instead of shortstop), Stop-Fix, and Bleach-Fix. Times and temperatures are available from Agfa dealers. The developer is isothermal, that is, it will provide equivalent results at different temperatures if the processing time is changed to agree with the temperature used. Mix the chemicals the day before you plan to begin work.

Printing with three separate exposures has two disadvantages in comparison with the 'white light' method. The filters must be removed and new ones placed on the filter tray in darkness. In addition local control of exposure (burning in and dodging) must be planned and done proportionately for each color.

The advantages are that only three filters need be purchased and these are small inexpensive gelatin filters for use beneath the lens. Also much more sensitive color control is possible. And in addition color theory and practice can be learned more thoroughly and with great speed.

Before attempting to print a naturalistic scene photographed with color negative, it is desirable to investigate the nature of the color process and of the colors available with the process. The following program will develop great skill in handling the materials and also encourage a sensitivity to the color itself before these are linked to the production of a naturalistic image. With color, as with monochrome, there are two kinds of response to the picture. One is to the color statement itself. The other is to the subject in front of the camera. Gaining a sense of control of the color before applying it to a total relationship of subject and color is helpful.

The color photogram is an excellent tool for learning color printing and also yields useful images. With 'white light' exposures, a photogram is essentially a monochromatic statement, although it has a definite color cast unless the exposure is exactly the right one to produce a neutral tone. With three-color exposures a very rich color statement is possible and the relationships between primary exposures is soon understood. Examine Figure 5-6. Imagine you have placed a block of wood on a piece of color print material. With the red filter in place make exposure 1. The rest of the paper has been exposed to red light. This will produce cyan dye in one layer of the paper. The area under the wooden block will remain clear.

RED exposure = Cyan dye

Move the block a little, to position 2. Replace the red with the green filter. Make a second exposure, to green light. This will produce magenta dye, in areas *e* and *c*. Area *e* already has cyan dye, so the magenta will add to that. Area *c* was clear, so it will now have only magenta.

GREEN exposure = Magenta dye

Replace the green filter with the blue. Move the block to the lower left. Expose for blue light. Area *e* now has magenta + cyan + yellow dye and will approach a black tone (the color and density of this will be determined by the balance and amount of the three exposures).

BLUE exposure = Yellow dye

Area *a* will have cyan + yellow. Cyan has blue + green components. The yellow and blue will make a green; and the net color of area *a* will be green. Area *d* will have cyan + magenta. Magenta has blue + red components; cyan has blue + green components. The red and green will add to form a neutral density, leaving a blue component. Therefore area *d* will appear blue. Area *b* will have been protected from exposure to two of the primary sources but not to the blue light that forms a yellow dye. Thus area *b* appears yellow. Area *f* has been protected from all light and remains white.

Suppose that an exposure to produce a neutral black (determined by trial and error) required 20 seconds of red light. This could be produced by breaking that into 5 exposures of 4 seconds each. If the block were moved a little between each exposure, the shape would be a series of cyan images, stepping from dark to light. If the green and blue exposures were similarly broken up into small pieces, the color possibilities in the overlapping areas become very complex.

Any opaque shape or substance can be used to create negative shapes in color in this kind of photogram. It can be left in place, or moved between primary exposures. A translucent substance will add its texture and a negative of its inherent color to the image.

After making several photograms to accustom yourself to handling the materials, filters, and processing in total darkness, attempt printing a conventional black-and-white negative as a black-and-white print, using the color printing paper. To do this successfully requires sensitive control of the three exposures. Achieving a neutral print will build a sense of understanding of the process. Since the negative has complimentary colors relative to the' print colors, the following relationships hold:

INCREASING the negative exposure in:	will INCREASE the print density in:
RED	cyan
GREEN	magenta
BLUE	yellow

DECREASE the negative exposure in:	if the print is EXCESSIVE in:
RED	cyan (blue-green)
Red + Green	blue
GREEN	magenta (purple)
Green + Blue	red
BLUE	yellow
Blue + Red	green

Correct exposures can be achieved easily if the principle of bracketing exposures is used. If the first print is too dark, attempt to make the next print definitely too light. If you achieve this, then the third try can "split the difference" between the first and second exposures, and be close to a correct print. Attempting to "creep up" on a correct exposure by making tiny corrections is tedious and wasteful of materials.

If a trial print is too yellow (a common fault in beginning printing) make the next print too blue: decrease the blue exposure by one-half. If this produces a print with cold blue highlights, then you have established the correct region of exposure and can estimate an increase of blue for the third print that will be close to the correct color.

The Agfa print material appears when wet much the same as it does when dry. There are changes, however. The dry print is about 1/3 to 1/2 stop darker than the wet print and a little more yellow (or less blue). For critical printing let the print dry and examine that before making a final print.

Three-color exposures will require a very accurate timing device. Probably the best available is provided by HEATHKIT; it should be supplemented by an automatic voltage control transformer. These are supplied by SOLA and WESTON as "automatic voltage regulation" transformers. This device prevents voltage variations from changing the brightness, color temperature, and timing of the enlarger lamp and the electronic timer, both of which are sensitive to voltage changes.

Experimental, non-standard color negatives can be printed with three-color printing directly, and without difficulty. White-light printing requires a very complicated and dense filter pack for printing Ektachrome processed in negative materials to produce a non-standard color negative. Such a negative can be printed with the three-color method with the same directness as a conventional negative. Or composite prints involving both color and monochrome images on the same paper can be done by printing three-color instead of white light.

OTHER COLORING METHODS

Color may be applied to the print. A traditional color medium has been oil paint. This has been used in a dilute form for emulating naturalistic color for many years. Color was applied to the surface of the print in the earliest history of photography. Lately there has been new interest in applied color, not so much for emulating naturalistic color as to reinforce the print character of the photograph and introduce another dimension to the response.

Oil paints may be applied to the surface and they bond well. Dye may be painted into the gelatin. Dr. P. H. MARTIN dyes are excellent; vivid, clear, and with excellent penetrating and adhesive power. Color spotting dyes are also made by Kodak.

Areas which you wish to color may be masked by painting the boundaries with rubber cement. After drying, the cement is carefully buffed off. This undoubtedly also results in sulfur contamination and a shorter life expectancy for the print. Colors may be formed chemically . EDWAL provides a series of color developers that produce strong colors on silver prints through chemical action.

Dye transfer images may be made and combined with black-and-white prints. Follow the KODAK Dye Transfer Process, except that the final transfer is made onto conventional paper. Agfa Portriga Rapid works well. Brovira will work too, except the color will bleed laterally unless the print is rapidly dried after the last transfer is finished. Print the black-and-white images first, fix and air-dry the paper, then treat it in mordant and transfer the dye image where desired.

Color gum and silkscreen images can be combined with platinum, ferrocyanotype, gravure, and conventional silver images for other possibilities.

BIBLIOGRAPHY

Adams, Ansel	**Basic Photo Series** (Vol. I-V) New York: Morgan and Morgan
Arnheim, Rudolf	**Art and Visual Perception** Berkeley: U. of California
Gernsheim, Helmut and Alison	**A Concise History of Photography** New York: Grosset & Dunlap
Perls, Hefferline, Goodman	**Gestalt Therapy** New York: Delta Books
Ivins, William M., Jr.	**Prints and Visual Communications** Cambridge: M.I.T Press
Klee, Paul	**The Thinking Eye** New York: George Wittenborn & Company
Morgan, Willard, ed.	**Photo Lab Index** New York: Morgan and Morgan
Neblette, C.B.	**Fundamentals of Photography** New York: D. Van Nostran
Newhall, Beaumont	**The History of Photography** New York: Museum of Modern Art
Todd, Hollis, and Zakia, Richard	**Photographic Sensitometry** New York: Morgan and Morgan
White, Minor	**Zone System Manual** New York: Morgan and Morgan
	Some Methods for Experiencing Photographs, **Aperture 5:4, 1957**
	Mirrors, Messages, Manifestations New York: Aperture
Winters, Yvor	**Forms of Discovery (Introduction)** Swallow Press: Chicago
	In Defense of Reason *(Anatomy of Nonsense; The Significance of 'The Bridge' by Hart Crane) Chicago: Swallow Press.*